GET SKINNY!

THE ORGANIC WAY

Eating your way to a stronger, leaner, healthier you.

Andrew J. Fox HHP, MS, CSCS

GET SKINNY! THE ORGANIC WAY
EATING YOUR WAY TO A STRONGER, LEANER, HEALTHIER YOU.

iUniverse books may be ordered through booksellers or by contacting:

iUniverse
1663 Liberty Drive
Bloomington, IN 47403
www.iuniverse.com
1-800-Authors (1-800-288-4677)

ISBN: 978-1-4917-6290-5 (sc)
ISBN: 978-1-4917-6291-2 (e)

Library of Congress Control Number: 2015903882

Print information available on the last page.

iUniverse rev. date: 08/25/2016

ANDREW FOX

Andrew J. Fox is the founder of TrueLife Fitness & Wellness, Inc., a corporation that for the last 15 years has offered personal training, nutritional counseling and wellness coaching. He holds a degree as a Holistic Healthcare Practitioner, a B.S. in Sports Management with a minor in Fitness and Wellness, a Masters in Exercise Science and Health Promotion, is a Certified Personal Trainer, Certified Strength and Conditioning Coach and a Performance Specialist. His education matches his experience to bring results to his clients. Andrew is an advisory board member and consultant for non-profit cancer organizations, the UCLA Psychology and Oncology departments, as well as other well-known clinics and schools. He is a Director for the National College of Exercise Professionals, teaching and certifying health professionals for top fitness facilities. His clientele includes professional athletes, cover models, celebrities, as well as a broad spectrum of people of different ages and needs, from rehabilitation and weight loss to performance and sports specific training. Author of *Balanced Life*, Andrew cares about each and every person he works with. By utilizing the proper foundations of health, exercise and wellness, he educates and motivates his clients to achieve true health--the health we were designed and created to enjoy. For more information on Andrew Fox or TrueLife Fitness & Wellness, Inc. please visit his website at truelifefitness.us.

NICOLE OCHOA

Nicole Ochoa is an accomplished fitness trainer, athlete, actress and humanitarian who embodies the full notion of "living life to its fullest." A native of Los Angeles, Nicole was a student athlete at UCLA and after attaining her degree in sociology turned her passion for health and fitness into first a stint as a professional wrestler and stuntwoman and for the past 16 years as a NASM-certified personal trainer and fitness model. During much of that time, Nicole has also been engaged with the entertainment community both in front of the lens as a member of the Screen Actors Guild and behind the camera as writer and producer. Nicole's life would not be complete without her devotion to those less fortunate and toward that end she has worked tirelessly with the Special Olympics, the homeless throughout Los Angeles, and orphans around the world including personal humanitarian and spiritual visits to Brazil, Africa, Israel and Guatemala. You may contact her at nicoleochoa.com

CONTENTS

DEDICATIONS

Thanks to God for any and all insight, wisdom, and desire to help and encourage others.

Thanks to my Mother and Father for giving me every ounce of love and support.

Special thanks to my Mother who helped me with the cooking and baking, and for her experience and advice. I see how fortunate you are to have been brought up on a farm and to have learned how things should be properly grown, raised and prepared.

Thanks to the clients who made it all possible, the Usell family, who provided the idea for this book, encouraged me to share my knowledge with others, and their endless belief and support in my passions. I am so blessed that God brought you all into my life. May I be the same blessing to you.

To every person who has ever looked for the right way to be fit and feel great. I wanted to call the book TRUE NUTRITION after my nutritional company because this is the way to health. Use it as a guide and follow it as closely as you can. Take the 3-month *Get Skinny (GS) Challenge*, and you will love how you look and feel. You will learn how easy it is to cook healthy meals and help our environment at the same time.

Protein Packed Granola pg. 6

Parfait pg. 7

Muesli pg. 5

Smoked Salmon with Eggs pg. 16

BBC Breakfast Bake Casserole pg. 20

Simple Chewy Cereal Protein Bars pg. 8

INTRODUCTION

Get the body you've always wanted, TRULY.

The GET SKINNY cookbook is about achieving your best body through good nutrition. The ultimate goal is to get you HEALTHY so that you can get the lean, toned, muscular, athletic, vibrant, and beautiful body that you have always wanted. This is the way your body **wants** to be and how you were **created** to be. We were meant to eat food as close to nature as possible: whole, fresh, organic. The following recipes are intended for adults, children, seniors, and anyone who wants to achieve health in its truest form. It is a new way of living that will lead you to not only loving the way you look, but the way you feel.

For the best results, make the recipes as described or use them as guidelines to make your own. Feel free to add a little more of this or less of that, and to make them your own. Just make them healthy by using the highest quality fresh, local, organic ingredients that you can find. By choosing natural ingredients, you are benefitting your health, your digestive system, your metabolism and the Earth that gave us all of these wonderful things to eat and enjoy.

Being a Nutritionist, a Certified Personal Trainer, Strength and Conditioning Specialist, I created these recipes for true results no matter what your goals are. These are close to the recipes that I make professionally for clients. Over the years I have refined them to obtain the perfect balance of nutrition to achieve their goals.

We want this cookbook to introduce you to a world of cooking and creating healthy food that once was a part of everyone's lives. We want to help you take charge of what you choose to eat and to take ownership in how it's prepared. This will empower us to get the best out of our minds and bodies. Cook for yourself, your family, and loved ones, and give the gift of your time and health to yourself and others! GET SKINNY! The Organic Way.

To Get Skinny--We Need To Get Healthy

It's really not about getting skinny but getting healthy. "Getting Skinny" is a byproduct of being healthy. Over the years, society has conditioned us to be lazy when it comes to food, slaves to convenience, being sold tasty food and treats with little to no real nutritional value. This reality is impairing the health of this wonderful creation that is the truly amazing human body. We are designed to be strong, vibrant and healthy, able to withstand illness and disease and able to thrive under almost any condition.

As a health professional working in this field for many years as a Nutritionist and Holistic Healthcare Practitioner, I believe that half of our diseases can be cured by our diet. Talented physicians, from Dr. Weston Price, Dr. Mercola, Dr. Hyman, Dr. Day, Jordan Rubin, and even Hippocrates and Pythagorus, to name a few, all understood that nutrition is the key and the foundation to health and wellbeing. Food with little to no nutritional value has caused our country to become the leader in obesity, heart disease, cancer and diabetes, now commonly known as "Western diseases." We are suffering from preventable diseases in this country because we are entrusting our health to the food industry and restaurants, but they are more interested in your dollar than in your health. They spend billions of dollars to get you hooked on their fast, convenient, highly addictive junk food. Modern day convenience foods are extremely low in nutritional value and are designed to "hook" you at first bite, so that you will keep coming back. Before you know it, it's an unhealthy habit that is not easy to break. Convenience gets you in the door, and the high fat, sugar and salt keeps you coming back for more--until you get the news about your obesity, high cholesterol, blood pressure, heart disease, diabetes, and even cancer. We must be vigilant about our health, learn about our bodies and what they need to be healthy, learn more about our food, and how it is grown and prepared. By planning, shopping, experimenting and cooking, you will be creating new habits that will lead you to amazing results and a stronger, healthier you over time.

To Get Skinny - Eat Organic

I have clients who have lost significant amounts of weight simply by starting to eat organic. Your body desires real food – properly balanced, fresh, whole, unprocessed, and as close to nature as possible. This book gives you what your body needs to achieve what's been eluding you, true health and real results. The more pure, natural and wholesome the food you eat, the more it raises your metabolism. Processed foods are stripped of nutrients and are difficult for your body to digest, lowering your metabolism making it hard to lose weight. Worst of all, they are designed to make you want more of the same creating an unhealthy, unhappy habit that keeps you from getting results. Digestion is how your body absorbs and assimilates nutrients. Up to 65% of your daily energy is devoted to digestion. Fresh, organic, wholesome foods are easier for your body to digest and more nutritionally dense. You will absorb more nutrients from these higher quality foods. Natural, wholesome foods do not create the unnatural cravings that processed foods do. Giving your body what it really wants and needs from properly balanced organic foods as close to nature as possible, in the proper balance, will yield tremendous results, both in how you look and how you feel.

Do you know what your grandparents called organic food? **Food.**

Non-organic foods starve your body of nutrients and load your system with unnatural toxins. The toxic pesticides, herbicides, fungicides, hormones, antibiotics, genetically modified organisms (GMO's), artificial colors and flavors, and processed foods lead to the most prevalent diseases and disorders in the country, ruin your digestive system, slow your metabolism and make you FAT.

In the last few decades our food has changed significantly. The modern American diet is filled with processed foods that have all sorts of chemicals, pesticides, growth hormones, antibiotics, and pollutants. These toxins are not good for the environment or for our bodies, and they are causing you to be overweight. The toxins in your food contribute to weight issues and obesity, and disrupt the function of our hormonal system leading to disorders such as heart disease, diabetes, obesity, and high cholesterol. Recently the American Medical Association has finally come out in support of the idea that these toxins and pollutants play a significant role in our national obesity crisis.

What qualifies as organic?

Simply stated, organic produce and other ingredients are grown without the use of pesticides, synthetic fertilizers, sewage sludge, genetically modified organisms, or ionizing radiation. Animals that produce meat, poultry, eggs, and dairy products do not take antibiotics or growth hormones. The USDA National Organic Program (NOP) defines organic as follows:

Organic food is produced by farmers who emphasize the use of renewable resources and the conservation of soil and water to enhance environmental quality for future generations. Organic meat, poultry, eggs, and dairy products come from animals that are given no antibiotics or growth hormones. Organic food is produced without using most conventional pesticides; fertilizers made with synthetic ingredients or sewage sludge; bioengineering; or ionizing radiation. Before a product can be labeled "organic," a Government-approved inspector inspects the farm where the food is grown to make sure the farmer is following all the rules necessary to meet USDA organic standards. Companies that handle or process organic food before it gets to your local supermarket or restaurant must be certified also.

GMOs are another issue altogether.

Genetically modified organisms, or GMOs, are plants or animals created through the gene splicing techniques of biotechnology (also called genetic engineering, or GE). This experimental technology merges DNA from different species creating unstable combinations of plant, animal, bacterial and viral genes that cannot occur in nature or in traditional crossbreeding. This is not considered safe by 60 other countries in the world, and these countries have completely or substantially banned GMOs.

Asking for organic is why we are seeing more organic items being sold across the United States. Every time you purchase an organic item you are voting. Why vote organic?

By choosing at least one organic product out of every 10 items you purchase…

- 915 million animals would be treated more humanely
- You eliminate 2.5 million pounds of antibiotics used in livestock each year
- 25,800 square miles of degraded soils would be converted to rich, highly productive cropland
- 98 million servings of water would be free of toxic pesticides each day

- 53 million servings of produce would be produced without toxic pesticides each day
- 20 million servings of milk would be produced without synthetic hormones or antibiotics each day
- 2.9 billion barrels of imported oil would be eliminated each year
- 6.5 billion pounds of carbon would be captured in the soil

The Organic Center: **www.organic-center.org**

Organic is more of an educational challenge, than a financial one.

–Miguel Rivera,
the Organic Farmer

To Get Skinny--Give Your Body What It Needs

The key to health in all things is balance, and your nutrition is no different. The recipes in this book focus on the building blocks of health, giving you the proper balance of fruits and vegetables, protein, carbohydrates, and fats in each meal. My main focus with all of my clients is QUALITY.

This is where you become proactive about your health. We want quality, but we don't want to pay for it. You may have heard the true saying, "You can pay for your health now, or pay for it later." Find the best possible resources for food. If your local big box grocer is all you have, make the best choices available there. I travel often and have to do the best I can with what I have. There will be trial and error as you learn, but be cognizant of your choices and always buy the healthiest food you can give your body. What good is Getting Skinny! if you get heart disease, cancer or diabetes? Let's look at the long haul, not the quick trip to health.

Once you have quality, then we strive for BALANCE. This is not easy today. With Paleo diets, gluten free, vegetarian diets, Atkins, Mediterranean, etc. it is easy to become very confused by focusing on our food rather than on what our bodies actually need. Our bodies desire a balance of carbohydrates, both low and high glycemic, proteins, wild and grass fed, and healthy fats. To purchase a full customized nutritional program which will define what ratios of each macronutrient work best for your gender, age, body size and type and individual goals, visit our website at truelifefitness.us. This program will take your body and your health to the next level!

Every recipe in this book is designed to help you Get Skinny, Build Muscle and Lose the Fat

To Get Skinny--Focus on Foundations Not Fads

As a nutritionist, I see so many people running to the newest supplement, herb, extract, or super food, being promoted by a supposed health professional getting paid a gross amount of money to tout this new and unfound elixir of weight loss, muscle gain, memory enhancer, etc. I teach the basic foundations of health and ask such questions as, are you eating the daily recommended amount of fruits and vegetables? Do you eat whole, unprocessed carbohydrates and high quality wild, grass fed organic proteins? Do you get enough sunlight, sleep and exercise regularly? The answer is always NO. We are all looking for that magical quick fix THAT JUST DOESN'T EXIST. Focus on the foundations. Why spend a tremendous amount of money on a newly found supposed super food that has not been proven? Spend money on what is proven and makes sense, organic food that you were meant to eat. As we learn about preparing quality food and eating it in the proper balance, make sure to get enough water and exercise. Let's embark on a new path to true health. Now let's get cooking…

First, my challenge to you. Make health a habit. The required training is below…

To Get Skinny--Get Up and Cook

We have all fallen for modern conveniences and shortcuts, but how convenient are they when they impair your health? What do you think our ancestors would say if they saw how we have succumbed to the cheap and tasty? My grandmother and mother would spend hours cooking for their families, fresh, wholesome healthy foods they would prepare directly from the farm. Learning more about nature, where our food comes from and how to prepare healthy meals is just pages away.

"When you have the best and tastiest ingredients, you can cook very simply and the food will be extraordinary because it tastes like what it is."

- Chez Panisse

Your Get Skinny Challenge? Making Health and Cooking a Habit

Changing your eating habits will be one of the most important things you'll ever do for yourself. While processed foods are cheap, quick, and abundant, whole foods require a little more effort but will yield amazing results in both your mind and body. Take the time and do the work, the more you do it the easier it gets, the more you do it the better the result, and you have just created a healthy habit.

Get the bad food out. Get the family and friends involved, it is essential to have good food in the house at all times. Treat bad food as an unwelcome guest. The first thing to do is to rid your kitchen of all of the garbage. If it's there, you'll eat it.

Start Here:

- Plan to make one or two meals this week.
- Plan what you want to make and write a shopping list of what you will need.
- Make larger portions so you only have to cook a few times each week.
- Have a designated shopping day (or two) and a designated cooking day (or two), spend an hour shopping and an hour cooking. It takes time and practice, but you will be surprised at how easy we made this for you.

Your next step:

- Spend one week eating only what you cook completely from scratch. Just one week will have you feeling better and looking better. For one week use only single organic ingredients: flour, rice, oats, organic milk and yogurt, grass-fed meat, organic fruits and vegetables, and basic pantry supplies (yeast, baking soda, etc.) Include your kids in the process of making homemade foods. (If they're included in the preparations, it helps to lessen the complaining if they are craving foods that are more familiar.) Even if your diet is already pretty clean, you may be surprised to discover that you have more of a reliance on non-organic, packaged, processed items than you thought.

- Many people are put off by the high price of eating healthy, and they are right to a certain extent. If you go to the health food store and buy packages of organic crackers, fancy breads from the bakery, and other gourmet items, you will spend a fortune. Keep in mind that an organic processed food is still a processed food. It's better than something from Kellogg's or General Mills, but it isn't ideal. There are a lot of ways to clean up your diet without breaking the bank. You should only be buying single organic ingredients: flour, rice, oats, organic milk and yogurt, grass-fed meat, organic fruits and vegetables. Be sure to check out your local farmers' market to find a local food at a great price.

- Another of the major complaints about a whole foods lifestyle is that it is too time-consuming. I have you covered! I know that you are busy, but your health is worth it. There will be a learning curve, but with proper planning, you will find that I have designed these meals to not only be delicious, but simple, easy, and best of all quick! Being sick and unhealthy is far more expensive and time-consuming than taking a moment to prepare a Get Skinny! meal or snack.

Once you cut the toxic, processed foods from the majority of your diet, you will begin to notice how good you look, feel and function. When you go off-plan and eat a bag of chips or a fast food meal you will feel unwell. The interesting thing about this is that you felt that way ALL THE TIME before cutting that food from your diet, but you didn't realize it because feeling unwell was your normal baseline.

Grab an apron and take charge of your health and your life! (I'll meet you at your local organic grocer...)

Yours Truly,
Andrew

THE BASICS: HOW TO USE THIS BOOK

Everyone rides a rollercoaster of health, the question is, how much? We want to lessen the rise and fall of that rollercoaster and teach your body to have more control, giving it consistency which will stabilize and improve your health and get you results.

Start Here:

Start slow. My first goal for you is to implement 3 GS! recipes per week, and one additional each week until you are up to 2 GS! meals per day.

- If you currently eat 1 meal per day, your goal is 2-3 GS! meals per day. (We call these times Breakfast, Lunch, and Dinner!) People who eat one or two meals a day are typically eating too much food at one time, and usually not the right kind of food. This will overload your metabolism and make you store fat.
- If you currently eat 2 meals per day, your goal is 3 meals (of which 1-2 would be GS! meals). If you are an active woman or athlete, add one snack or meal.
- If you are a male and eating 3 meals per day, that is fine with me, try to make 2 GS! meals. If you are a larger man in stature, or you are active you can go up to 3-4 meals per day.

The ultimate goal is to change how you eat and to make you responsible for your health through what you eat. Eating every day the GS! way is ideal. Focus on quality.

Custom tailored nutritional programs are available through my company and performed by professional nutritionists. These will define what ratios of each macronutrient work for your gender, age, body size and type and individual goals, as well as your micronutrients, sugars, fiber and electrolytes. Visit our website at truelifefitness.us for more information. This program will take your body and your health to the next level!

Plan ahead what meals you will be making and what foods you will be buying at the beginning of the week.

Your next step
One day per week, make it your…

<u>Get Skinny! Day</u>
(Or GSD… for short)

…the Organic way. Plan a day to have only GS meals.

Not cooking at all? Your goal is to make 1 - 2 meals per week.

Cooking once or twice a week? Your goal is to make 3 - 4 meals per week, and 1 GS! Day. Start by planning your first one, then plan 1 or 2 the next week…

You cook 3 – 4 times per week? Start making 2 - 3 GS! Days per week.

It's a process, a lifestyle, a new way of living, plan it, and then plan on how you will progress.

Start cooking with family and friends, kids and husbands, wives and neighbors. Food brings people together, use these recipes for your health and the health of others, and so much more. Just start.

READY TO GET COOKING?

* Blender and food processor (optional but recommended)
* Wooden or metal spoons, large
* 9x13 baking sheets (2)
* 8x11 casserole dish (glass is easier to clean)
* Muffin pans and loaf pans for breads
* 12-16" frying pans with lids
* Large 5 qt. pan with lid or wok for larger dishes
* Skillet for pancakes
* Stew pots for soups (3 qt. and 6 qt.) with lids
* Pasta pot/colander with lid
* A few good knives for cutting and chopping
* Whisk
* Rubber spatulas
* Spatula to turn eggs
* Pot holders
* Tongs
* Small or medium sized sieve with handle for rinsing
* Measuring cups and spoons
* Mixing bowls
* Resealable Pyrex bowls, various sizes
* Food scale, digital or analog
* Spices: sea salt and black pepper, garlic, oregano, basil, cumin, paprika, cinnamon, thyme, rosemary and onion are a great start. You can use blends, such as Mexican seasoning or taco seasoning, just make sure that they are all spices and contain no salt/sodium.

A QUICK NOTE, to all users. If you are not able to get a certain item that the recipe calls for, **GET AS CLOSE AS YOU CAN AND DO THE BEST YOU CAN WITH WHAT YOU HAVE.**

Example: Recipe calls for dry sprouted oats, and all you have access to is the Quaker guy. It's all good, get as close as you can for optimal results.

Adjustments for Vegetarian: Use eggplant, sprouted organic tofu, tempeh, or seitan for proteins. For Gluten Free options: Use gluten free breads, pastas, chips and tortillas.

GS! Healthy Hummus pg. 33

Fruit Salad and Fruit Plate pg. 30

Pico De Gallo pg. 29

Vegetable Platter pg. 32

Superbowl Nachos pg. 47

Asian Chicken Lettuce Wraps pg. 31

Chicken Salad pg. 64

BREAKFAST

The most important meal of the day? Absolutely.

Rule #1: Always buy organic, whenever possible

You get what you pay for. Whenever it comes to your health or wine, always buy the best.

GS! POWER-FULL SHAKE

Pre or post workout or for a snack, these shakes taste great and will fuel your energy, muscle and fat loss

SERVES 1

Method

Toss all ingredients in a blender with some ice if desired, blend and enjoy!

Ideas: Frosty Vanilla Peach, Very Berry with chocolate or vanilla protein, Chocolate Almond Butter Banana

Nutrition facts per serving: Calories 243, Carbohydrates 33g, Protein 20g, Fat 5g

Choose your adventure:

First, choose a protein: 1 serving of whey or vegetarian plant-based Plain, Chocolate or Vanilla flavor to inspire your shake. You may substitute 1 serving of plain Greek low fat yogurt if you'd like.

1 c. fruit, fresh or frozen, tropical fruit, berries, bananas, etc.

1 heaping tsp. fat, coconut oil, almond butter, flaxseed meal, hempseed or chia seed meal

¼ c. raw oats (for athletes)

8-12 oz. water (the GS! way!), low fat milk, unsweetened almond, rice or coconut milk

PROTEIN OATMEAL WITH FRUIT AND NUTS

This is my mom's morning staple, so I tweaked it for optimal health benefits...

SERVES 1

½ c. dry sprouted oats

½ c. water

½ c. 2% milk

½ c. fruit, I use sliced apples but berries or bananas are great too...

⅛ cup nuts, chopped (small handful) or try 1 tsp of your favorite nut butter stirred in (it's fantastic) (optional)

1 heaping tbsp. vegan vanilla protein powder, or Goatein by Garden of Life

1 tsp. cinnamon

Method

Combine oats, water and milk in a small or medium sized cook pot and turn heat to medium high, let cook for 5 minutes

Stir in nuts and protein powder, and top with fruit and a few dashes of cinnamon

Let cool and enjoy

Nutrition facts per serving: Calories 367, Carbohydrates 48g, Protein 22g, Fat 11g

MUESLI

For a great, nutritious quick breakfast at home, office or on the go, I recommend Muesli

SERVES 1

Method

Combine ingredients and mix together

Enjoy!

Nutrition facts per serving: Calories 353, Carbohydrates 63g, Protein 16g, Fat 5g

1 serving (6-8 oz.) plain low fat yogurt
½ c. raw oats (¼ c. for women)
1 c. fresh or ½ c. dried fruit (I use berries or berry mixes)
1 tsp. raw honey (optional, unless on GS! program)
1 tsp. cinnamon

PROTEIN PACKED GRANOLA

Perfect for a snack by itself, or with yogurt (see parfait). For kids, sometimes I'll add some dark chocolate chips after granola is baked and cooled... (unless on the GS! program)

SERVES 15

2 ½ c. sprouted oats

1 c. your favorite dried fruit (I use a mix of dried blueberries, cherries and pineapple)

¾ c. of your favorite organic nuts, chopped or sliced (I use a mix of pecans, almonds, and sunflower seeds)

½ c. vegan vanilla protein

¼ c. raw honey

1 tbsp. coconut oil

2 tbsp. cinnamon

1 tsp. vanilla

½ tsp. salt

Method

Preheat oven to 300

Warm coconut oil into liquid form (I put it in the oven for a minute or two in a stainless steel measuring cup)

Mix together all ingredients, except dried fruit, until all oats are coated and everything is combined, use a mixer if necessary

Line a rimmed baking sheet with a piece of parchment

Spread mixture onto baking sheet

Bake for 30-35 minutes, stirring mixture around on baking sheet every 5-10 minutes

Let cool, add dried fruit and mix together

Store in airtight container

Nutrition facts per serving: Calories 159, Carbohydrate 24g, Protein 6g, Fat 5g

PARFAIT

A great, healthy way to serve breakfast to guests and family, looks and tastes great!

SERVES 1

Method

In a bowl, jar or glass, layer ½ of the yogurt on the bottom, then ½ of the granola, then ½ of the berries, repeat

Add a few dashes of cinnamon to each layer

Nutrition facts per serving: Calories 358, Carbohydrate 59g, Protein 17g, Fat 7g

1 serving GS! Protein Granola (see recipe)

1 c. fresh berries (I use strawberries and blueberries)

1 serving (6-8 oz.) plain low fat yogurt

A few dashes of cinnamon

SIMPLE CHEWY CEREAL PROTEIN BARS

Something for the kids, and you!

SERVES 15

¾ c. raw honey

3 scoops vanilla vegetarian protein powder

¾ c. nut butter

¾ c. applesauce

1 10 oz. box crisp rice or flake cereal

½ cup of your favorite dried berries, cranberries, raisins, blueberries, cherries, etc.

Method

Preheat oven to 350

In a large stainless steel or oven safe bowl, or even casserole dish, mix honey, protein, nut butter and applesauce together and put in the oven for 6 minutes or so, until mixture is heated and almost all liquid

Take bowl out with care, it will be hot

Stir and mix together

Add cereal and stir thoroughly until cereal is coated

Stir in dried fruit

Spray a 9x13 dish or pan with non-stick spray and using a spatula press mixture evenly into dish

Refrigerate and cut into bars

Nutrition facts per serving: Calories 227, Carbohydrate 36g, Protein 8g, Fat 7g

PERFECT PROTEIN PANCAKES OR WAFFLES 5 WAYS

Simple, healthy, delicious. I Make a quick stack and eat them plain, and pack them for lunch, probably have some on me right now. Yes, I share.

SERVES 4

TIP: Going Gluten Free? Going Vegan? Alternatives: Want waffles? Just pour batter into a waffle maker instead, the "5 ways" still applies.

1 ½ c. sprouted whole grain flour, or quinoa or oat if going gluten free
½ c. vegetarian vanilla protein
1 ½ c. low fat milk, or rice/hemp milk if going vegan
1 egg
¼ c. applesauce
1 heaping tbsp. raw honey
3 tsp. baking powder
1 tsp. coconut oil
1 tsp. vanilla extract
½ tsp. salt

Method

Mix all ingredients together

Heat skillet or pan to medium heat and spray with all natural spray, such as coconut oil or sunflower oil spray

Pour 3 tbsp. (a little less than ¼ c.) batter in skillet or pan

Brown on both sides until batter is done, plate and spray skillet again before adding more batter

If they start to get too brown turn the heat down a bit

Nutrition facts per serving: Calories 216, Carbohydrates 27g, Protein 15g, Fat 3g

5 Ways to the Perfect Protein Pancake...

The first basic way is my favorite, featured above. Be creative and have fun! To make blueberry pancakes, I use 1 c. of fresh or frozen blueberries. After pouring batter, allow it to cook for 2 minutes or so, sprinkle blueberries onto the uncooked top, allow to cook for another 2 minutes or so, and then flip. Allow pancake to cook and you will have yourself some amazing blueberry protein pancakes!

3 more...

Try: using ½ c. of organic dark chocolate chips, some banana slices and ¼ c. walnuts, apple slices and cinnamon

Nutrition Facts for above dark chocolate chip and banana walnut (apple cinnamon will be the same as blueberry), per serving: Calories 345, Carbohydrates 39g, Protein 15g, Fat 12g

**Rule #2: Do not limit your creativity,
just watch out for adding too
much fat, sugar or sodium**

These recipes are guidelines for you to learn how to make good food, the healthy way, but also for you to expand your new talent and grow. Try new things, but also be mindful that it is easy to lose track of how much sugar, fat or sodium we are <u>really</u> using. These things will affect your GS! results.

SCRAMBLED EGGS & VEGGIE SCRAMBLE

A simple nutritious breakfast! To make scrambled eggs, just omit the vegetables and cheese. Start the day off right, with 2 servings of vegetables per serving!

SERVES 2

4 slices sprouted whole grain
   bread, lightly toasted
3 eggs
3 egg whites
1 tbsp. low fat milk or milk
   alternative (plain almond,
   hemp or rice milk)
½ c. mushrooms, chopped
½ c. fresh or frozen spinach
½ c. green pepper, chopped
½ c. fresh or frozen broccoli
½ c. red onion, chopped
3 cloves garlic, minced
¼ c. mozzarella or low fat cheddar,
   shredded
1 tomato, sliced
Sea salt
Black pepper

Method

Spray and heat a skillet or pan on medium high heat

Add garlic, mushrooms, spinach, onions, peppers and broccoli and sauté for a few minutes

In a bowl beat together eggs and milk

Pour into skillet and cook until eggs are set

Mix in cheese and serve with toast, placing sliced tomatoes on top

Nutrition facts per serving: Calories 418, Carbohydrates 44g, Protein31g, Fat 15g

GS! EGG SANDWICH

A pre-workout powerhouse!

SERVES 1

TIP: Wilting spinach – lightly spray a pan with cooking spray and set on medium heat, toss a handful of spinach into the pan and add 1 tbsp. water, cook for a few minutes until spinach wilts

Method

Split muffin in half and lightly toast in toaster. If you don't have a toaster place muffin cut side down in pan once warm and press to toast, should be a couple minutes for each muffin side

Spray a pan with cooking spray and let pan warm up on medium heat

Cook egg in pan for a few minutes then flip over with spatula to cook until done, seasoning with a light dash of salt and pepper

Take muffin from toaster and place bottom half on a plate with cheese on top, when egg is done place egg on cheese and cook bacon until crisp

When cooked, place bacon onto egg, then tomato slices, wilted spinach, red onion slices and finally your sprouts

Nutrition facts per serving: Calories 374, Carbohydrates 30g, Protein 31g, Fat 15g

1 sprouted whole grain muffin or 2 slices toast
1 egg or 2 egg whites
2 slices turkey bacon
1 slice Swiss cheese or low fat cheddar
2 slices tomato
2 slices red onion
Handful of spinach, wilted
Sea salt
Black pepper
Sunflower sprouts (optional)

BREAKFAST TACOS

Healthy Mexican breakfast at its GS! best.

8 corn tortillas
1 potato, cooked or baked, cut,
    quartered and chopped
4 eggs
4 slices turkey bacon, cooked and
    chopped
2 c. frozen spinach
½ onion, sliced
½ c. shredded mozzarella
½ c. fresh salsa (see Pico de Gallo
    recipe under SIDES)
Sea salt
Black pepper

Method

Heat a large pan or skillet over medium heat, once hot, add 1 tbsp. ghee

Add onions and let them cook for a few minutes before adding your spinach and eggs

Once spinach and eggs have been added let them cook for 4-5 minutes and the add potatoes and lightly season with sea salt and black pepper

Once eggs are almost fully cooked add cheese, bacon and stir everything together, remove from heat

Place 1 tortilla on a plate and spoon eggs mixture onto tortilla

Top with 2 tbsp. of fresh salsa

Nutrition facts per serving: Calories 351, Carbohydrates 38g, Protein 23g, Fat 12g

OH MY GS! OMELET

So easy, even YOU can do it! Use any vegetables that you would like, or none at all. We want to show you the basics so you are in charge and you can take it from there. Feel free to double the recipe to make for 2.

SERVES 1

Method

Spray a pan with cooking spray and put on medium low heat

In a bowl mix eggs and milk

Once pan is hot add egg mixture and tilt pan so egg mixture covers the bottom evenly

When omelet begins to firm, add cheese and vegetables to one half

Use a spatula to fold and cook until bottom is golden brown

Remove and plate, serve with toast

Nutrition facts per serving: Calories 239, Carbohydrates 17g, Protein 20g, Fat 9g

1 egg
2 egg whites
1 tbsp. milk or milk alternative
¼ c. shredded mozzarella or low fat cheddar cheese, crumbled goat or feta are a nice touch too
¼ c. red onion, chopped
¼ c. mushrooms
¼ c. fresh spinach
1 slice cooked turkey bacon, diced (optional)

SMOKED SALMON WITH EGGS

Just like lox and eggs... with vegetables, hello skinny...(health)

SERVES 2

4 slices Ezekiel toast
2 eggs and 2 egg whites
2 oz. smoked salmon, diced
1 slice Swiss or low fat cheddar
    cheese
4 slices tomato
2 large slices red onion
Handful spinach
Sea salt
Black pepper

Method

Heat a large pan on medium heat and spray with cooking spray

When pan is hot, add eggs to pan and scramble

After a few minutes cooking add cheese, salmon, and then spinach and continue to scramble while cooking until eggs are done

Either plate and top with tomato slices and red onion, with toast on the side or make egg sandwich

Nutrition facts per serving: Calories 339, Carbohydrates 30g, Protein 28g, Fat 11g

FRITTATA

One of my favorites, because you can really pack in the vegetables while keeping the taste. Use any variation of vegetables that sounds good to you. Serve with toast, or toss 1 c. cooked quinoa into the mix.

SERVES 4-6

Method

Set oven to 350 or if you don't have an oven safe pan, follow directions below

Heat a pan on medium heat and lightly coat with cooking spray

Once pan is hot, sauté your vegetables for 4-5 minutes, if using bacon, you can cook your bacon in the pan at the same time

In a large bowl, blend eggs, cheese and ½ tsp. of both salt and pepper

Pour egg mixture into pan and let cook until bottom and sides start to firm

Using a spatula, lift the sides and tilt the pan all around the frittata to allow uncooked egg mixture in to cook

When it looks well-cooked all around, either put it in the oven, or place a lid on top and turn heat to low, allowing it to cook for 10 minutes

3 eggs + 4 egg whites
2-3 garlic cloves, minced
½ c. red onion, chopped
½ c. mushrooms, chopped
½ c. broccoli, asparagus, zucchini or spinach
1 large tomato, sliced
2 strips turkey bacon, diced (optional)
1 oz. (¼ c.) parmesan, grated
1 bunch fresh parsley
Sea salt
Black pepper

Remove from heat and loosen sides and bottom with spatula

Place a large plate over pan and flip over

Place sliced tomato and parsley on your frittata, cut and serve with toast

Nutrition facts per serving: Calories 179, Carbohydrates 13g, Protein 17g, Fat 6g

SPINACH BACON FETA WRAP

You may also use English muffins or just plain toast if you'd like and make little egg bacon feta sandwiches, delicious, so easy and so healthy! Please feed to your children with love.

SERVES 4

Method

Spray cooking pan and sauté garlic on medium heat for 2-3 minutes before adding eggs

In a separate pan, spray and start to cook bacon as directed, usually also on medium heat

Let eggs cook for a minute or two and then add all of the vegetables except for the tomatoes

Add salt and pepper (a nice pinch of each should do) cover with lid, stirring occasionally for 6-8 minutes

Place tortillas open on a plate, one tortilla per plate and using a large spoon scoop eggs and vegetables onto tortilla, add 1-2 slices of bacon, 2-3 tomato slices and about 1 oz. (¼ c.) of crumbled feta

Roll up and enjoy

Nutrition facts per serving: Calories 289, Carbohydrates 27g, Protein 19g, Fat 13g

4 whole grain tortillas
4 eggs + 4 egg whites
8 slices turkey bacon
1 bag of fresh or frozen spinach (preferably fresh, if frozen thaw and squeeze out excess water)
3-4 oz. feta, crumbled
1 large tomato, cut in half and then sliced (option, used sundried tomatoes :)
1 box mushrooms, sliced
1 zucchini, cut in half lengthwise and sliced
3 garlic cloves, minced
Sea salt
Black pepper

BBC BREAKFAST-BAKE-CASSEROLE

A great dish when serving friends or family, or to make and have throughout the week.

SERVES 12

1 lb ground turkey or tempeh
1 onion, finely chopped
1 bell pepper, finely chopped
1 c. fresh or frozen spinach
10-12 slices of sprouted whole
   grain bread, I use Ezekiel, cut
   into 1" square pieces
½ c. Gruyere cheese, grated
3 large eggs
4 egg whites
2 ½ c. low fat milk
1 ½ tbsp. fresh chives, chopped
Sea salt
Black pepper

Method

Preheat oven to 350

Spray a large pan or skillet and place over medium heat

Once pan is hot, add ground turkey, onions, bell pepper, and spinach

Cook and stir until the turkey is cooked through, about 8-10 minutes

Add about ½ tsp. of both salt and pepper to the turkey and vegetables

Spray a 9x13 casserole dish with non-stick spray

Add the bread to the casserole dish it should be a layer or two, then add your turkey and vegetables and stir them in

Sprinkle evenly with the cheese

In a bowl, whisk together the milk, eggs, and chives and pour over the bread, turkey and vegetables and stir them together, making sure that everything is even and coated

Bake in oven for 45-55 minutes, remove and let cool, cut and serve

Nutrition facts per serving: Calories 278, Carbohydrates 27g, Protein 26g, Fat 7.5g

Rule #3: Believe

You're an intelligent person, you bought this book, know that doing the right thing the first time will never bite you in the end. Believe that you can get healthy, skinny, buff, whatever, as long as your goal is aligned with true health. Believe that eating food as close to nature as possible, in the proper balance will leave you looking a lot better, and a lot healthier. It's all here in this handy little book of cooking wonders… Seriously.

NANCY'S FABULOUS FRENCH TOAST

You will love this recipe, my mom makes a double batch and keeps them in the fridge, just pop in the toaster and it's like they just came off the stove...

SERVES 4

½ loaf sprouted grain bread, about 8-10 slices
2 eggs and 4 egg whites
2 tsp. vanilla
1 tbsp. cinnamon
½ tsp. salt
1 ½ c. low fat milk

Method

Mix ingredients together well with a whisk and pour into a 9x13 baking dish or pan

Heat frying pan to med heat and spray with cooking spray or use 1-2 tsp. ghee or coconut oil

Lay bread in mixture for 30 seconds or so and flip with a spatula to soak for another 20-30 seconds, adding more bread to mixture as you take soaked bread out to fry

Cook French toast for a few minutes on each side, until golden brown

Enjoy with turkey bacon, eggs and/or fruit, or just by themselves!

Nutrition facts per serving: Calories 264, Carbohydrates 35g, Protein19g, Fat 6g

MMMMMM— MUFFINS (3 WAYS! AT LEAST?)

So easy, I like to let kids do this one so they can see that cooking delicious and healthy is easy!

SERVES 12

Method

Preheat oven to 350

Combine all ingredients together, except fruit and whisk together until smooth

Add fruit (and nuts if using nuts) and stir to combine

Spray a muffin tin with non stick spray, and using a tablespoon, spoon mixture into muffin tin

(I do 2-3 heaping tbsp. per muffin space)

Bake for 20 minutes, remove from oven and let cool in tin for 5 minutes

Remove muffins from tin and place on rack to completely cool

Serve or freeze

Nutrition facts per serving: Calories 145, Carbohydrates 24g, Protein 4g, Fat 3g

2 c. sprouted whole grain flour
½ c. low fat milk
2 large eggs
1 ⅓ c. fresh or frozen fruit (mashed banana, blueberries, diced apple, etc. Are you limiting yourself? Well, stop it!)
⅓ c. + 1 tbsp. raw honey
⅓ c. unsweetened applesauce
2 tsp. baking powder
½ tsp. baking soda
1 tsp. vanilla extract
½ tsp. sea salt
¼ c. nuts, chopped (optional)
1 tsp. cinnamon

MY TRUE NUTRITION HUEVOS RANCHEROS

A family favorite, Mexican, the Get Skinny! way!

SERVES 4

Salsa (or Pico de Gallo)
4 eggs
1 16 oz. can black beans
1 bunch cilantro, chopped
1 package corn tortillas
1 oz. (¼ c.) crumbled feta or goat cheese
Garlic seasoning
Sea salt
Black pepper

Method

Heat a pan on medium heat

Start with Salsa:

Use store bought fresh salsa (or see Pico de Gallo recipe in Snacks & Starters section)

1 tsp. olive or grapeseed oil or cooking spray

Fry salsa 3 minutes then remove to bowl

Add a light sprinkle of salt and pepper

Rinse beans and add to the same pan, add a few sprinkles of garlic seasoning and ½ c. water

Cook over low heat until warmed and smash slightly with a fork, remove to another bowl

Cook eggs any style and season with a dash of salt and pepper for each egg

Warm tortillas in the same pan, 30 seconds to 1 minute per side

Place each tortilla on plate, add black beans, then cooked egg, salsa, sprinkle cheese, and cilantro

Nutrition facts per serving: Calories 251, Carbohydrates 30g, Protein 17g, Fat 8g

SNACKS AND STARTERS

Rule #4: Have Fun

Because I said so! Cooking and creating fabulous, healthy and tasty dishes is fun. Remember art class? Now you're in charge... and you're so much more fun to be around, when you're having fun.

GUACAMOLE

Avocado. The butter pear, restaurant style

SERVES 4

Method

Cut avocados in half, remove pit and scoop out avocado and mash in a bowl with a fork

Add tomatoes, onions, cilantro, squeeze ½ lime, salt and pepper

Mix and serve

2 ripe avocados, cut in half, pitted and scooped out and mashed with a fork
1 tomato, diced
½ white onion, diced
½ lime, juiced
3 tbsp. cilantro, chopped
½ tsp. sea salt
Dash black pepper

QUICKER AND EASIER GUACAMOLE

It just doesn't get easier than this...

SERVES 4-6

2 avocados
½ - ¾ c. Roasted Salsa Verde

Method

Mix and serve

Nutrition facts per serving: Calories 142, Carbohydrates 12g, Protein 3g, Fat 11g

PICO DE GALLO

I mix this up every few days and have it on, well... everything

SERVES 4

Method

Mix together in a bowl, and enjoy

Nutrition facts per serving: Calories 28, Carbohydrates 7g, Protein 1g, Fat 0g

2 large tomatoes, chopped
½ onion, chopped
1 jalapeno, chopped (optional)
½ lime, juiced
¼ c. cilantro, chopped
Sea salt
Black pepper

FRUIT SALAD & FRUIT PLATE

Healthy balanced, summer specialty

SERVES 8

Choose any of your favorite fruit and use a nice array of colors. I use:

2 c. strawberries, sliced
1 c. blueberries
3 kiwi's, sliced
2 c. grapes

2 c. melon of choice, in cubes or balls
1 c. low fat cottage cheese or plain low fat yogurt

Method

Either toss fruit together in a large bowl and serve separately in small bowls with a dollop of low fat cottage cheese or plain low fat yogurt, OR

Arrange fruit on a large dish or platter with a bowl of low fat cottage cheese or yogurt in the center for dipping

Nutrition facts per serving: Calories 79, Carbohydrate 15g, Protein 5g, Fat 1g

ASIAN CHICKEN LETTUCE WRAPS

A great snack or starter

SERVES 4

Method

Lightly spray a large skillet or pan and place over medium heat, once hot add oil

Place chicken in pan and let cook for 5-6 minutes, stirring often

Add garlic, ginger and onions to pan and continue to cook. Stir for 4 minutes

Add water chestnuts, hoisin sauce and a dash of both salt and pepper, continue to cook for a few more minutes

Lay 1 or 2 lettuce leafs stacked 1 on top of the other open on a plate and using a spoon or tongs, spoon chicken and vegetables onto center of the lettuce leafs

Pour some of the sauce over the chicken and vegetables and sprinkle green onions on top

Nutrition facts per serving: Calories 115, Carbohydrates 5g, Protein 15g, Fat 4g

2 boneless, skinless chicken breast or 4 thighs
VEGAN ALTERNATIVE: Seasoned tempeh, chopped into 1-2" pieces
½ c. hoisin sauce
1 onion, sliced
2" fresh ginger, minced
4-5 cloves garlic, minced
2 -3 green onions, sliced
1 can water chestnuts or ¼ c. chopped cashews
1-2 tsp. sesame oil
Sea salt
Black pepper

VEGETABLE PLATTER

Low cal snacking at it's best, get those vegetables every chance you get!

SERVES 6

Choose any of your favorite vegetables, use a nice array of colors, I use:

1 bag baby carrots
2 large heads of broccoli, cut
1 head cauliflower
1 box of cherry tomatoes
1 large cucumber, sliced

Method

On a large dish or tray, arrange vegetables

Serve with our hummus or dill dip recipe

Nutrition facts per serving: Calories 49, Carbohydrate 5g, Protein 3g, Fat 1g

GS! HEALTHY HUMMUS

Hummus is a great snack and appetizer, and it goes great with vegetables

SERVES 8

Method

Combine all to a food processor and blend for a few minutes, stir around and blend again. Store in re-sealable container and refrigerate.

Variations! Try adding 1 tsp. cumin if you like the spicy Mexican flavor, or paprika, or try adding a handful of pitted Kalamata olives, or 1 roasted red pepper, 1 tsp. lemon juice, 2 garlic cloves, 1 tsp. tahini, ⅛ c. water, 1 tsp. paprika and 1 tsp. chili flakes roasted red peppers!

Nutrition facts per serving: Calories 105, Carbohydrates 11g, Protein 4g, Fat 5g

4 garlic cloves
½ tbsp. olive oil
1 can of garbanzo beans, or purchase dried garbanzo beans and soak overnight, rinse and they are ready to use (I personally recommend this, sprouting makes their nutrients more bioavailable and easier to digest)
½ c. tahini
⅓ c. lemon juice
1 tsp. sea salt
Parsley, minced to top (optional)

WHITE BEAN AND BASIL HUMMUS

A personal favorite

SERVES 8

1 14 oz. can white cannellini beans (drained and rinsed)
¾ c. fresh basil tightly packed or ⅓ c. dried
¼ c. fresh parsley (optional, but recommended)
1 lemon, juiced
3 garlic cloves, minced
1 tbsp. olive oil
⅓ c. tahini
A pinch of sea salt
A pinch of black pepper

Method

Mix all ingredients in a blender, food processor, or by hand, first mashing beans well in a bowl with a fork and then incorporating the rest of the ingredients into the mix

Mix/puree until creamy, occasionally scraping sides

Nutrition facts per serving: Calories 86, Carbohydrates 7g, Protein 3g, Fat 5g

OUR BABA'S BEST DILL DIP

My grandmother was an amazing cook... maybe that's where I get it from...

SERVES 6

Method

Mix ingredients together

Refrigerate for an hour or 2 to get best flavor

Enjoy with vegetables

Nutrition facts per serving: Calories 57, Carbohydrates 3g, Protein 8g, Fat 2g

2 c. low fat plain Greek yogurt
2 tsp. lemon juice
2 tsp. onion, minced or grated
1 tsp. sea salt
1 tsp. dry mustard (I have found that regular mustard works too)
½ tsp. dry dill weed

SPICY BLACK BEAN DIP

1 c. black beans cooked on a skillet
   w/ ¼ c. water til warm and
   mashed with a fork
1 c. low fat plain Greek yogurt
¼ c. onion, diced
¼ c. bell pepper, diced
½ tsp. garlic powder
½ tsp. cumin
½ tsp. sea salt
½ tsp. black pepper
½ tsp. chili pepper
¼ c. tomato, diced for the top or
   Pico de Gallo (see recipe)

Method

After mashing black beans, I usually just add the yogurt, vegetables and seasoning right to it and mix with a wooden spoon right in the pan or skillet

Use a rubber spatula to scoop into a bowl, refrigerate or serve

Nutrition facts per serving: Calories 70, Carbohydrates 10g, Protein 6g, Fat 1g

BRUSCHETTA

A great appetizer

SERVES 16

Method

Heat a large skillet or pan on medium heat and pour 1 tbsp. olive oil into pan, along with 2 chopped garlic cloves, stir

Once pan and oil are hot and you can smell the garlic cooking, place bread slices into pan to grill or toast lightly for a minute or two, and then turn, grilling the other side, then when both sides are done, remove from heat to a large plate

Pour your other tbsp. of oil into pan, along with the other chopped garlic, and diced tomatoes, stir and sauté for 2-3 minutes, then remove from heat, you may keep them in the pan

In a bowl, stir ricotta, basil, lemon juice, salt and pepper together

Spread one side of the Italian bread slices with your ricotta cheese mixture, then spoon on your tomatoes

Refrigerate for 10 minutes, then serve

Nutrition facts per serving: Calories 89, Carbohydrates 11g, Protein 4g, Fat 3g

1 loaf Italian bread, cut into 1" thick slices (about 16)
3 large tomatoes, diced
2 tbsp. olive oil
1 c. ricotta, part skim milk
¼ c. basil leaves, chopped
1 tsp. lemon zest
4-5 garlic cloves, minced
1 tsp. both sea salt and black pepper

ROASTED BRUSSELS SPROUTS

Great with chicken or steak, rice and/or potatoes, and of course a large salad ☺

SERVES 6

1 ½ lbs. Brussels sprouts
1 ½ tbsp. olive oil
1 tsp. sea salt
½ tsp. black pepper

Method

Preheat oven to 400

Mix all in large bowl

Place Brussels sprouts on baking sheet and bake for 35-40 minutes

Nutrition facts per serving: Calories 62, Carbohydrates 6g, Protein 3g, Fat 3g

ZUCCHINI PANCAKES

I'll make a batch just to have around, a great balanced snack or appetizer

SERVES 9

Method

In a large bowl, combine all ingredients and mix together, combining thoroughly

Spray a large skillet or pan and heat on medium high heat

Using a tablespoon, spoon out 2 heaping spoonful's of zucchini pancake mix onto your skillet for each pancake

Cook for a few minutes, and turn

Plate and serve with low fat plain Greek yogurt for dipping

Nutrition facts per serving: Calories 104, Carbohydrates 10g, Protein 8g, Fat 4g
(2 pancakes per serving)

- 1 ½ lb. or 5 zucchini squash, finely chopped, processed or grated
- 2 cloves garlic, minced
- ½ onion, chopped
- 4 eggs
- ¾ c. flour
- ¾ c. 2% milk
- ⅓ c. parmesan, grated
- 1 tsp. baking powder
- 1 tsp. Italian seasoning
- 1 tsp. both sea salt and black pepper
- Nonfat plain Greek yogurt for dipping

PERFECT POPCORN

Great for movie night!

SERVES 4

½ c. white or yellow popcorn kernels

1-2 tsp. coconut, ghee (clarified butter), or sesame oil (depending on what flavor you're going for)

Mexican spices, Italian spices, Chinese spices (usually sold as a blend)

Method

In a large pan or skillet with lid (preferably glass) on medium high heat, melt oil in pan and spread it around by holding the handle of the pan and tilting the pan different directions (up, down, side to side)

Once oil is hot and melted, pour kernels into pan and keep close to heat shaking and moving pan in a back and forth motion, you will hear/see the kernels start to pop, keep shaking and moving the pan until the popping of kernels becomes less frequent

Toss with fresh lime juice, sea salt and thyme if using coconut oil

Toss with sea salt and Mexican spices if using sunflower oil

Toss with sea salt and Chinese spices if using sesame oil

Toss with sea salt if using ghee

Nutrition facts per serving: Calories 142, Carbohydrates 25g, Protein 4g, Fat 4g

POWER-FULL SHAKE

Pre or post workout or for a snack, these shakes taste great and will fuel your energy, muscle and fat loss

SERVES 1

Method

Toss all ingredients in a blender with some ice if desired, blend, and enjoy!

Ideas: Frosty Vanilla Peach, Very Berry with chocolate or vanilla protein, Chocolate Almond Butter Banana

Nutrition facts per serving: Calories 243, Carbohydrates 33g, Protein 20g, Fat 5g

Choose your adventure:

First, choose a protein, 1 serving of whey or vegetarian plant based Plain, Chocolate or Vanilla flavor to inspire your shake. You may also use 1 serving of plain Greek low fat yogurt if you'd like.

1 c. fruit, fresh or frozen, tropical fruit, berries, bananas, etc.

1 heaping tsp. fat, coconut oil, almond butter, flaxseed meal, hempseed or chia seed meal

¼ c. raw oats (for athletes)

8-12 oz. water (the GS! way!), low fat milk, unsweetened almond, rice or coconut milk

PROTEIN PACKED GRANOLA

Perfect for a snack by itself, or with yogurt (see parfait). For kids, sometimes I'll add some dark chocolate chips after granola is baked and cooled... (unless on GS! Program)

SERVES 15

2 ½ c. sprouted oats
1 c. your favorite dried fruit (I use a mix of dried blueberries, cherries and pineapple)
¾ c. of your favorite organic nuts, chopped or sliced (I use a mix of pecans, almonds, and sunflower seeds)
½ c. vegan vanilla protein
¼ c. raw honey
1 tbsp. coconut oil
2 tbsp. cinnamon
1 tsp. vanilla
½ tsp. sea salt

Method

Preheat oven to 300

Warm coconut oil into liquid form (I put it in the oven for a minute or two in a stainless steel measuring cup)

Mix together all ingredients, except dried fruit, until all oats are coated and everything is combined, use a mixer if necessary

Line a rimmed baking sheet with a piece of parchment

Spread mixture onto baking sheet

Bake for 30-35 minutes, stirring mixture around on baking sheet every 5-10 minutes

Let cool, add dried fruit and mix together

Store in airtight container

Nutrition facts per serving: Calories 159, Carbohydrate 24g, Protein 6g, Fat 5g

PARFAIT

A great, healthy way to serve breakfast to guests and family, looks and tastes great!

SERVES 1

Method

In a bowl, jar or glass, layer ½ of the yogurt on the bottom, then ½ of the granola, then ½ of the berries, repeat

Add a few dashes of cinnamon to each layer

Nutrition facts per serving: Calories 358, Carbohydrate 59g, Protein 17g, Fat 7g

1 serving GS! Protein Granola (see recipe)
1 c. fresh berries (I use strawberries and blueberries)
1 serving (6-8 oz.) plain low fat yogurt
A few dashes of cinnamon

GRANOLA BARS

Far healthier and better balanced than anything I have seen out there... Great for school lunches, after school, bike rides or road trips

---

SERVES 15

1 ¾ c. sprouted oats
½ c. vegan vanilla protein
1 c. your favorite dried fruit (I use dried blueberries, pineapple and dates)
¾ c. your favorite nuts, chopped or sliced (I use sunflower seeds, almonds and pecans)
3 ripe bananas
1 egg or 2 egg whites to lower fat GS Program
2 tbsp. cinnamon
1 tsp. vanilla extract
½ tsp. salt
Handful dark chocolate chips (optional, unless on GS! Program)

Method

Preheat oven to 350

In a medium sized bowl mash and mix your bananas, with the egg and vanilla

In a large bowl combine all of your other (dry) ingredients

Add banana mixture to your dry mix and stir it all together so everything is evenly coated

Spray a 9x13 baking pan with non stick cooking spray and press mixture into pan making a thin layer

Bake for 15 minutes, remove from oven and let cool in pan, cut and enjoy

TIP: Not sweet enough? Try adding 1 tbsp. raw honey to the mix (not for GS!)

Nutrition facts per serving: Calories 145, Carbohydrates 22g, Protein 6g, Fat 5g

Rule #5: Exercise is your new best friend.

Don't you dare call the publishing company complaining that you aren't seeing results if you are intaking alcohol beyond reason, or not following the program to its full potential. Here's the other part of the program that will give your body all the right curves, energize you when done properly, and make you feel amazing. Three days per week <u>minimum</u>, you go out… all out, and test the limits of that awesome creation, your human body. Take it for a swim, a jog, some yoga, a workout, then test your limits, push, and hit the gas a little…

Just don't let the cops see you.

Proper exercise will accelerate fat loss, stimulate the metabolism, and build lean healthy, strong muscle. Hello results…

NO BAKE PROTEIN BARS

This is a popular recipe that I have seen many places, a great sweet healthier snack or treat for kids (and us ☺)

2 c. creamy almond butter, cashew butter or tahini
⅔ c. honey or maple syrup
½ c. applesauce
2 c. vanilla or chocolate whey protein powder (or mix vanilla and chocolate)
1 c. oats
½ c. flax, sesame or chia seeds

Method

Preheat oven to 375

In large glass bowl, mix nut butter, applesauce and honey. Set in oven until mixture is liquid form or close to

Stir, then add protein, stir, add oats, stir, add chia, stir

Cut and store refrigerated, makes 24 bars

Nutrition facts per serving: Calories 190, Carbohydrates 14, Protein 12, Fat 12, Fiber 3g

SUPERBOWL NACHOS

The healthiest and tastiest nachos you may ever eat...

SERVES 6

Method

Preheat oven to 325

Pile chips high on a large oven safe dish or pan

Drain and rinse black beans and then pour them over chips, distributing them evenly

Evenly distribute shredded cheese over the mountain of chips and beans

Place into the oven and bake until melted, about 10 minutes

Take dish out from the oven and top with shredded lettuce, diced tomatoes, green onions, sour cream or yogurt, and finally top with black olives and avocado, sprinkle with cilantro

Nutrition facts per serving: Calories 284, Carbohydrates 28g, Protein 10g, Fat 13g

1 bag of sprouted tortilla chips, or make your own by cutting up your favorite tortillas into 2" squared pieces and bake in the oven at 325 until crisp

1 c. black beans, drained and rinsed

2 oz./½ c. shredded mozzarella

1 large head of iceberg lettuce, shredded

2 large tomatoes, diced

½ ripe avocado, peeled and cut into slices

3 heaping tbsp. of low-fat sour cream or plain Greek yogurt

Green onions, sliced

1 can or jar of black olives, chopped

1 bunch cilantro, chopped

Unbelievable BLT pg. 67

Chinese Chicken Salad pg. 53

Andrew's Mexican Salmon Sandwich pg. 73

Cobb Salad pg. 54

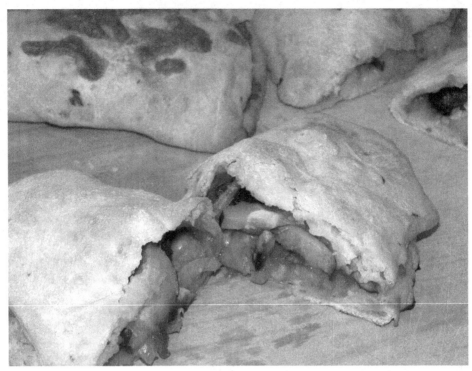

Pizza and Pizza Pockets pg. 78

Yellow Cake and Cupcakes pg. 156

LUNCHES & DINNERS

RULE #6: Make it look pretty

Food should be made to bring out its best, nutritionally, and aesthetically. Prepare food to look appetizing, be an artist with your dish.

- Getting Skinny starts with salad, but not just any salad…
perfectly balanced, organic salad/meals -

CHINESE CHICKEN SALAD

Salad is a great healthy meal, by making it a few different ways, it keeps things from getting boring, and hopefully will give you new ideas...

SERVES 4

Method

In a skillet or pan, on medium high heat, pour one tbsp. of sesame oil into pan. Sauté ginger and garlic for 2 minutes

Once hot, add chicken and cook for a 3-4 minutes, stirring occasionally

Add 2 tbsp. tamari to chicken and cook for another 3-4 minutes, until chicken is done, remove to plate

In a large bowl, combine cabbage, onions, carrots, chestnuts, and oranges

In a small bowl combine 2 tbsp. sesame oil, 4 tbsp. tamari and 1 tbsp. rice wine vinegar and whisk together

Pour contents of small bowl onto salad and mix together with noodles using tongs, large spoons, or your hands

Top with chicken and sprinkle with sliced almonds

Nutrition facts per serving: Calories 364, Carbohydrates 32g, Protein 25g, Fat 15g

2 large boneless, skinless chicken breasts, sliced into 1-2" pieces
1 head Napa cabbage, thinly sliced
½ head red cabbage, thinly sliced
Ramen noodles, cooked without seasoning
4 green onions, chopped
4 garlic cloves, minced
2" fresh ginger, peeled and minced
3 tbsp. Sesame oil
Tamari or soy sauce
Rice wine vinegar
1 large carrot, grated or shredded
1 – 10.5 oz. can Mandarin oranges
1 – 6-8 oz. can sliced water chestnuts
Sliced almonds

COBB SALAD
A restaurant favorite

SERVES 4

2 large boneless, skinless chicken breasts, cooked and chopped

3 heads of romaine lettuce, chopped

3 tomatoes, diced

4 slices of turkey bacon, cooked and chopped

1 medium sized avocado, peeled and sliced into small cubes

½ c. feta cheese crumbles

1 loaf fresh bread from bakery, sliced

Sea salt and black pepper for seasoning

Method

Arrange chopped romaine equally in 4 bowls

Start on one end, laying avocado down, then a line of tomatoes, then your chicken, then feta, and finally your chopped bacon

Season with a few dashes of sea salt and pepper

Serve with a slice or two of fresh bread

Nutrition facts per serving: Calories 381, Carbohydrates 32g, Protein 33g, Fat 13g

SALMON SALAD

A super healthy salad, high in omega 3's

SERVES 4

Method

Line up 4 bowls. In each bowl, add 2 c. spring mix, then top with tomato slices, red onion, avocado, a small sprinkle of feta, then your salmon fillet on top

Squeeze about a tsp. of lemon juice over each salad and season with sea salt and black pepper

Line the sides of each bowl with 1 serving of crackers

Nutrition facts per serving: Calories 407, Carbohydrates 33g, Protein 32g, Fat 14g

4 sockeye salmon fillets, fresh or frozen, baked and seasoned with sea salt and black pepper

8 c. spring mix salad

3 tomatoes, sliced and cut in half

1 medium avocado, peeled and cubed

1 red onion sliced

½ c. feta cheese crumbles

1 pkg of whole grain crackers, to serve on the side or to crumble over salad

1 lemon

Sea salt

Black pepper

BBQ CHICKEN SALAD

BBQ goodness, in a salad... you can also try using steak

SERVES 4

2 boneless and skinless chicken breasts, brushed with BBQ sauce, cooked in oven, then chopped

3-4 heads of romaine, chopped

1 – 15 oz. can black beans, drained and rinsed

1 – 15 oz. can whole kernel corn, drained and rinsed

½ c. shredded mozzarella

2 tomatoes, diced

1 red onion, chopped

2-3 green onions, chopped

1 bunch cilantro, chopped

2 servings of corn tortilla chips

2 tbsp. ranch dressing

¼ c. BBQ sauce (half for coating the chicken, and half for the dressing)

Method

Place chicken in the oven and cook for 25-30 minutes at 350

Or to grill, preheat the grill for high heat and lightly oil the grill grate. Once hot, place chicken on the grill, brush with BBQ sauce and cook 6 minutes, then flip and repeat. Cut into breast and make sure that chicken is fully cooked and that juices run clear. Remove from heat, cool, and slice

In a large bowl, mix romaine, tomato, cilantro, corn, onions, cheese, and black beans. Top with the grilled chicken slices and some crushed tortilla chips

In a small bowl, mix the Ranch dressing and BBQ sauce. Serve on the side or toss with the salad to coat

Nutrition facts per serving: Calories 421, Carbohydrates 45g, Protein 30g, Fat 13g

TRULY TANGY TACO SALAD

Truly a quick, easy favorite

SERVES 6

Method

Cook beef, turkey or tempeh and season with spices. Toss all ingredients (except cheese, avocado and chips) together in a large bowl. Mix the cheese and chips in last, top with avocado

Nutrition facts per serving: Calories 416, Carbohydrates 49g, Protein 29g, Fat 12g

16 oz. 93% lean ground beef, turkey (recommended), or tempeh
1 – 15 oz. can pinto beans
1 – 15 oz. can kidney beans
2 large tomatoes chopped
4 heads romaine lettuce, chopped
1 red onion, sliced
1 bunch green onions, chopped
1 medium avocado, sliced
½ c. shredded mozzarella or low fat cheddar
½ pkg. organic corn tortilla chips
1 tbsp. taco seasoning (add more to taste if needed)
½ tsp. each sea salt and black pepper

VERY VEGETABLE HUMMUS WRAP

Great for vegetarians, we chose to add grilled chicken or fish

SERVES 2

2 – 10" whole grain tortillas
1 large chicken breast or 6 oz. fish, cooked and sliced
1 tomato sliced and cut slices in half
2-3 romaine lettuce leaves
1 cucumber, julienned
2-3 carrots, julienned
1 small red onion, sliced
¼ c. hummus
½ c. sprouts
Sea salt
Black pepper

Method

Spread 2 tbsp. of hummus on ½ of each tortilla. To hummus side, add 3 oz. chicken or fish, tomato, cucumber, carrots and onion, finally topping it with lettuce and sprouts. Add a dash of sea salt and black pepper if desired

Fold bottom up an inch or two and roll into a wrap

Nutrition facts per serving: Calories 341, Carbohydrates 40g, Protein 25g, Fat 10g

CHICKEN CAESAR WRAPS

Light lunch or snack? Perfect for both!

SERVES 4

Method

Lay tortillas flat, one per dish, and spread a tsp. of dressing on half of each tortilla

Place 3-4 lettuce leaves and a few slices of chicken into each tortilla

Sprinkle lightly with 1 tbsp. of parmesan

Roll and cut in half, serve

Nutrition facts per serving: Calories 287, Carbohydrates 28g, Protein 25g, Fat 8g

2 large chicken breasts, boneless and skinless, cooked and sliced, seasoned with salt and pepper
4 large sprouted tortillas
Romaine lettuce leaves
Organic Caesar dressing
¼ c. shredded parmesan cheese
1 large tomato, sliced (optional)

YOUR BEST BASIC SANDWICH

SERVES 1

2 slices bread, lightly toasted

3 oz. of your favorite organic protein or vegan alternative - roast beef, turkey, chicken or tempeh, avocado, grilled portabella mushroom or eggplant

2 slices tomato

Alfalfa sprouts, any other sprouts are fine

Green leaf lettuce, as much as you can fit in!

Red onion, sliced

1 slice low fat cheese, mozzarella, Swiss, provolone, etc.

Mustard

TIP: Use organic sprouted grain bread, it's more nutritious and easier for your body to digest.

Method (In this order)

Bread
Mustard
Meat/Meat alternative
Lettuce
Red onion
Tomato
Sprouts
Cheese
Mustard
Bread

Nutrition facts per serving: Calories 367, Carbohydrates 40g, Protein 32g, Fat 9g

EGG SALAD & EGG SALAD SANDWICH

A classic

SERVES 4

How To Hard-Boil an Egg:

Place eggs in a sauce pan large enough to have them in a single layer, not stacked

Add cold water to cover the eggs by about an inch

Heat on high until water boils, cover the pan and simmer for about 10-12 minutes

Drain and let sit in cold water until you can easily peel

Serve warm or refrigerate

3 eggs, hard boiled
6 egg whites, hard boiled
3 tbsp. low fat mayonnaise
2 tbsp. plain low fat yogurt
½ tsp. sea salt
½ tsp. black pepper
Paprika if desired

Method

Hard boil all 9 eggs

Peel off egg shells and chop eggs (they do make an egg slicer usually available at most cooking stores)

Add yogurt and mayonnaise, a ½ tsp. of both salt and pepper, and mix together

Finish it off with a dash or two of paprika if desired

For sandwiches:

Lightly toast bread if desired and place a leaf or two of romaine or green leaf lettuce on top of your bottom slice of bread. Spoon in a serving of egg salad, top with another leaf or two of lettuce, and then add the top slice of bread

Nutrition facts per serving: Calories 117, Carbohydrates 2g, Protein 13g, Fat 6g

Nutrition facts per serving: Calories 277, Carbohydrates 32g, Protein 21g, Fat 7g
(As sandwich)

TUNA SALAD

Protein and veggie packed, with less than half the fat...

SERVES 4

Make your own healthier mayonnaise:

2 large eggs
1 tbsp. vinegar
½ tsp. salt
½ tsp. dry mustard
¾ c. extra-virgin olive oil
1 tbsp. lemon juice

Method

Mix ingredients together

Enjoy on a salad or on a sandwich on a bed of romaine or green leaf lettuce leaves

Nutrition facts per serving: Calories 150, Carbohydrates 6g, Protein 22g, Fat 4g

Nutrition facts per serving: Calories 310, Carbohydrates 36g, Protein 30g, Fat 5g
(As sandwich)

3 cans skipjack tuna, drained
3 tbsp. light organic mayo or make your own mayonnaise (see recipe)
3 tbsp. non fat Greek yogurt
3 stalks celery, chopped
1 medium onion, chopped
1 tsp. lemon juice
½ tsp. sea salt
½ tsp. black pepper

CHICKEN SALAD

Great on a salad, or between some slices of lightly toasted Ezekiel bread

SERVES 4

2 large boneless and chicken
    breasts, cooked and chopped
1 large apple, cored and chopped
1 c. grapes, sliced in half
¼ c. sliced almonds
2 tbsp. organic low fat mayo
3 tbsp. plain yogurt
2-3 green onions, sliced
1 tsp. lemon or lime juice
½ tsp. sea salt
½ tsp. black pepper

Method

Mix together all ingredients in a large bowl

For sandwiches:

Lightly toast bread if desired and place a leaf or two of romaine or green leaf lettuce on top of your bottom slice of bread, spoon in a serving of chicken salad, top with another leaf or two of lettuce, and then add the top slice of bread

Nutrition facts per serving: Calories 185, Carbohydrates 12g, Protein 17g, Fat 8g

Nutrition facts per serving: Calories 345, Carbohydrates 42g, Protein 25g, Fat 9g
(As sandwich)

TOASTED CHEESE

Comfort food for the waistline

SERVES 2

Method

Spray a pan or skillet with non-stick cooking spray and heat to medium heat

Slice cheese into 8 equal smaller slices

Lay bread on skillet and place 1 cheese slice on top (or spread feta) then add tomato slices and onions, top it off with ½ c. of your choice of vegetables and a dash of sea salt and pepper, add 1 more slice of cheese, then top with bread

Let grill for a few minutes or until cheese on the bottom is melted, then flip with care, grill until cheese on other side is melted

Cut in half and serve

Nutrition facts per serving: Calories 251, Carbohydrates 19g, Protein 19g, Fat 7g

4 slices of sprouted grain bread
1 tomato, sliced
½ red onion, sliced
1 c. vegetables, raw or lightly steamed (spinach, broccoli, bell peppers, etc.)
4 slices of mozzarella, Swiss, provolone, or 4 oz. feta
Sea salt
Black pepper

THANKSGIVING IN A SANDWICH

Get thankful

SERVES 4

Large turkey breast with skin
(about 12 oz.), lightly season
with salt and pepper, bake at
375 for 35 min or until done,
remove from heat and let
cool for 5 minutes or so, then
slice (NOTE: you may also use
chicken breast)
1 jar of cranberry sauce or
cranberry chutney
4 tsp. light mayo
1 head romaine lettuce
1 large tomato
8 slices turkey bacon, cooked
(optional)
4 slices Swiss cheese
1 loaf sprouted sourdough

Method

Preheat oven to 350

Lay bread on a baking sheet, and place 1 slice of cheese on the top slice of bread for each sandwich

Let bread toast in oven and cheese melt for about 5 minutes

Once cheese is lightly melted remove baking sheet and spread 1 tsp. mayo on bottom slice of bread

Add turkey, then cranberry sauce or chutney, then lettuce, 2 slices of turkey bacon, then 1-2 slices of tomato

Press together like Scooby and Shaggy making sandwiches in the cartoon

Cut in half and enjoy

Nutrition facts per serving: Calories 389, Carbohydrates 42g, Protein 31g, Fat 9g

UNBELIEVABLE BLT (IT'S TRUE...)

Dad's favorite, so I had to make it healthy

SERVES 4

Method

Lightly toast bread in the toaster, or if you'd rather, spread a small amount of mayonnaise on the outsides of the bread and lightly toast on a skillet, mayonnaise side down

Add cheese to lightly melt it

To assemble, start with toasted bread, spread with a small amount of mayonnaise

Add lettuce, tomato, bacon, avocado, more lettuce, a slice of cheese (if you didn't melt it on), and then top with another slice of toasted bread with mayo spread on the inside

Cut in half and plate

Nutrition facts per serving: Calories 363, Carbohydrates 36g, Protein 26g, Fat 15g

8 slices sprouted whole grain bread, lightly toasted
1 package turkey bacon, prepare as instructed on package
1 head green leaf lettuce
1 large tomato, sliced
1 avocado, sliced
Organic cheese slices (any white or yellow cheese will do, be creative and try gruyere, Havarti, Swiss...)
Mayonnaise
Sprouts (optional)

GS! SIMPLY HAMBURGERS

Does it get any easier than this?!

SERVES 4

1 lb. lean ground beef, you can also use venison, elk, turkey, or tempeh
1 pkg. of sprouted whole grain hamburger buns
1 egg
½ c. dried Ezekiel bread crumbs (leave a couple slices out to dry, or just toast them and crush into crumbs)
½ tsp. of both sea salt and black pepper

Toppings:
1-2 heads of green leaf lettuce
1 red onion, sliced
2 tomatoes, sliced
Sliced cheese, optional
Ketchup, Mustard, BBQ sauce, Hoisin sauce, whatever your pleasure!

Method

In a bowl, combine all ingredients together with your hands (except buns ☺)

Take ¼ of your burgers and roll up into a ball, then press it flat using the palms of your hands

Place on a plate to cook on the stove in a skillet, or on a sprayed baking sheet for the oven at 350 degrees, or on the grill!

Nutrition facts per serving: Calories 389, Carbohydrates 41g, Protein 35g, Fat 11g

PORTABELLA MUSHROOM BURGER & SANDWICH

You can also use eggplant

SERVES 2

Method

Use either a grill, a skillet, or a pan on medium heat

Mix together vinegar, oil, garlic and seasoning and coat mushrooms, save any extra for basting during cooking

Cook mushrooms for 5-7 minutes per side, starting with the top side down

Place cheese on mushroom top for the last minute of cooking

Nutrition facts per serving: Calories 240, Carbohydrates 38g, Protein 17g, Fat 5g

2 Portabella mushrooms
2 slices provolone
1 tbsp. olive oil
2 tbsp. apple cider vinegar
2 garlic cloves, minced
Italian seasoning
2 sprouted hamburger buns or 4 slices sprouted grain bread, toasted

Toppings:
1 head of green leaf lettuce
1 red onion, sliced
1 large tomato, sliced

BLACK BEAN BURGERS

A healthy vegetarian alternative, you can also use part black beans and part brown rice or quinoa

SERVES 4

1 - 16 oz. can of black beans or use
    sprouted black beans
1 bell pepper, minced
½ onion, minced
3 garlic cloves, minced
½ c. bread crumbs, or crushed
    dried Ezekiel bread
1 egg
2 tbsp. Mexican seasoning
Sea salt
Black pepper

Toppings:
4 slices provolone or mozzarella
1 head of green leaf lettuce
1 red onion, sliced
1 large tomato, sliced

Method

Pour beans into a large bowl and mash with a fork

Add bell pepper, onions, garlic, egg, seasoning and breadcrumbs and mix together

Using your hands, roll into 4 balls and shape into patties

Use a grill or bake in the oven at 350, cook for 8-10 minutes per side

Nutrition facts per serving: Calories 357, Carbohydrates 52g, Protein 21g, Fat 8g

TURKEY SURPRISE BURGERS

A favorite client of mine taught me to make these

SERVES 4

Method

In large bowl, mix all ingredients (except buns and cheese), make 8 small patties. Place cheese slice or shredded cheese in one patty and put another patty on top to enclose the cheese. Makes 4 burgers

Cook on grill or in skillet over medium heat, turning once (about 15 minutes)

Serve with bun, lettuce, tomato, and choice of condiments

Nutrition facts per serving: Calories 284, Carbohydrates 29g, Protein 26g, Fat 9g

1 lb. ground turkey
2 organic cheese slices, cut in half and folded over, or you can use shredded cheese (½ c.)
½ c. breadcrumbs
¼ c. finely chopped onion
1 egg
⅛ c. freshly chopped parsley
2 cloves garlic, minced
2 tsp. salt
1 tsp. pepper
4 sprouted hamburger buns

Toppings:
1 head of green leaf lettuce
1 red onion, sliced
1 large tomato, sliced

MAHI BURGERS

Why buy seafood burgers with fillers and sub par pieces of fish? Have fun with the family and make your own! Quick and easy, and oh so healthy! (Make a few extra for lunch the next day...)

SERVES 4

1 lb. Mahi, cross cut into small pieces (cross cut ½" squared or less)

⅓ c. cilantro, chopped

⅓ c. green onions, sliced

3 garlic cloves, minced

2 tsp. ginger, fresh or powdered spice

2 tbsp. hoisin sauce, tamari, teriyaki or soy sauce

2 tbsp. low fat mayo

1 tbsp. sesame oil

4 sprouted grain hamburger buns

Toppings:

1 head of green leaf lettuce

1 red onion, sliced

1 large tomato, sliced

TIP: Cut fish when it is still partially frozen, it is much easier to cut

Method

Combine all, except for sesame oil and freeze in a Ziploc bag or bowl for about 20 minutes, this will help emulsify the burgers so they will stick together

Remove from freezer, roll into balls and flatten

Heat a large pan or skillet to medium high heat and add oil

Once oil is hot, add burgers and cook for a few minutes on each side, then remove to plate

Toast buns in pan for about 30 seconds to a minute, then assemble burgers

Nutrition facts per serving: Calories 284, Carbohydrates 29g, Protein 26g, Fat 9g

ANDREW'S MEXICAN SALMON SANDWICH

This is seriously the jam. My personal favorite...

SERVES 4

Method

Preheat oven to 375

Cook bacon in pan according to directions

Sauté salmon (skin side down) on medium heat in the fat from the bacon to absorb the flavor

Cook for 5–7 minutes until cooked halfway through, turn over and season lightly with Mexican seasoning

Cook salmon for another 5–7 minutes until it flakes and place on a dish

Lightly coat ciabatta with mayonnaise and set in oven to lightly toast for 3-5 minutes

Assemble sandwiches, salmon, 2 slices bacon, tomato, avocado, red onion, then lettuce

Nutrition facts per serving: Calories 414, Carbohydrates 31g, Protein 35g, Fat 17g

1 large loaf of ciabatta (recommended) or fresh baked bread from Whole Foods cut in half and into 4 pieces (top and bottom of sandwich)
Fresh or frozen salmon 4 – 4 oz. pieces
8 slices turkey bacon, cooked
½ medium avocado, peeled and sliced
1 large tomatoes, sliced
1 red onion, sliced
4 tbsp. organic low fat mayonnaise or veganaise
1 head green leaf lettuce
Mexican seasoning

MOM'S ITALIAN CHICKEN SOUP

Soup, easy and healthy!

SERVES 6

6 c. chicken broth
2 c. water, enough to cover chicken
1 whole chicken, cut up or you may
    use 1 lb. of thighs or breasts
    (raw and chopped)
1 bag frozen spinach
1 large red onion, chopped
5 stalks celery, chopped
5 large carrots, chopped
1 box mushrooms, optional
4 garlic cloves, chopped
2 c. of your favorite pasta, we
    like the thick ribbon pasta or
    penne
1 tbsp. olive oil
½ tsp. each of basil, thyme, black
    pepper
½ c. parmesan, grated (optional for
    topping)
1 tsp. sea salt to taste

Method

Add everything into pot (except pasta and parmesan) and bring to a boil. Simmer for 25–30 minutes, stirring often, then de-bone chicken (if necessary)

Stir in pasta and cook until pasta is done

Serve and sprinkle with grated parmesan

Nutrition facts per serving: Calories 365, Carbohydrates 24g, Protein 36g, Fat 14g

GS! SLOW COOKER TORTILLA SOUP

After going out with my friends to many Mexican restaurants and seeing them order this dish, and then learning the nutritional facts, we resourced a base recipe from our chef and made a few adjustments... and then add a large salad for good measure

SERVES 4

Method

Place all ingredients in a slow cooker (except for lemon juice, tortilla chips, cheese and cilantro)

Cook on low to low medium heat for 6-7 hours, or on high for 3-4 hours. After cooking time is up, add lemon juice and stir

Plate and add tortilla chips, a sprinkling of cheese and some cilantro

Nutrition facts per serving: Calories 389, Carbohydrates 34g, Protein 28g, Fat 14g

3 chicken thighs, boneless and skinless
10 oz. can diced tomatoes with green chilies
15 oz. can black beans
2 c. chicken broth
1 c. water
1 onion, chopped
3 garlic cloves, minced
1 jalapeno, minced
½ tsp. cumin
½ tsp. chili powder
¼ lemon, juiced
4 servings of sprouted tortilla chips (1 serving per bowl) or tortillas
½ c. cilantro, chopped
½ c. Monterey Jack cheese, shredded

PEA SOUP

Great healthy soup, tons of GS! goodness...

SERVES 8

2 tbsp. olive oil
2 onions, chopped
5-6 carrots, chopped
5 celery stalks, chopped
2 cloves garlic, minced
2 cups dried split peas, yellow,
    green or mixed, rinsed
6 c. chicken broth
2 c. water
1 bay leaf
1 tsp. sea salt
½ tsp. black pepper
½ tsp. dried thyme
½ tsp. dried basil

Option: Try adding 6 slices of uncooked turkey bacon, sliced into small pieces, for added protein and flavor

TIP: Going vegetarian? Use vegetable broth instead of chicken broth

Method

In a large pot over medium high heat, sauté the oil, garlic, bay leaf, carrots, celery and onions for 5 minutes

Add peas, broth and water

Bring to a boil then reduce to low heat, partially covering pot, stir every 5-10 minutes

Simmer for about 30 minutes, then add basil, thyme, salt and pepper

Add bacon, if applicable

Simmer for another 30 minutes or until peas and vegetables are tender

Nutrition facts per serving: Calories 242, Carbohydrates 39g, Protein 14g, Fat 5g

LENTIL SOUP
Another great soup option

SERVES 6

Option: Try adding 6 slices of uncooked turkey bacon, sliced into small pieces, for added protein and flavor

TIP: Going vegetarian? Use vegetable broth instead of chicken broth

Method

In a large pot over medium high heat, sauté the oil, carrots, celery, onions and salt for 5 minutes

Add the rest of the ingredients and stir together

Bring to a boil then reduce to low heat, partially covering pot, stir every 5-10 minutes

Add bacon, if applicable

Simmer and stir occasionally for 40 minutes or until lentils are done

Nutrition facts per serving: Calories 172, Carbohydrates 34g, Protein 12g, Fat 5g

2 tbsp. olive oil
1 large onion, chopped
5 carrots, chopped
4 celery stalks, chopped
2 c. dried lentils, rinsed
2 tomatoes, diced
6 c. chicken broth
2 c. water
2 tsp. sea salt
½ tsp. coriander
½ tsp. cumin
½ tsp. black pepper

PIZZA & PIZZA POCKETS

The Get Skinny! Pizza and Calzone

SERVES 6

1 lb. fresh organic pre made pizza dough, or use recipe below

For Pizza Pockets: cut into 6 equally sized pieces, rolled into balls
½ c. pizza or pasta sauce
¾ c. shredded mozzarella cheese
4 cloves garlic, chopped
Your choice of vegetables and toppings: Choose 3
Turkey bacon
Turkey sausage
Shredded chicken breast
Pineapple
Spinach leaves
Zucchini
Artichoke
Red onion
Mushroom
Diced tomatoes
Black olives
Bell pepper
Eggplant
Broccoli
Green onions
Be creative!!!
Flour for sprinkling and rolling out dough
Fresh minced garlic
Sea salt and black pepper to taste

Keep it healthy, choose at least 3 vegetables and 1 protein option, or go all vegetables!

Method

Preheat oven to 375

Lightly flour a hard surface, counter, table, cutting board, etc.

Place 1 ball of dough on surface, lightly sprinkle some flour over it and knead or roll it out into a flat, round pizza crust

For Pizza:

Spread sauce, sprinkle cheese, add toppings

For Pizza Pocket:

In one half, spread a tbsp. or two of pizza sauce, then sprinkle some garlic, 2 tbsp. cheese and your choice of toppings (this should equal about ¾ c.)

Spray a baking sheet with non-stick spray and using a spatula, lay each pizza pocket onto baking sheet

Bake in oven for 15-20 minutes, until golden brown

Nutrition facts per serving: Calories 284, Carbohydrates 38g, Protein 16g, Fat 6g

How to make dough:

In a bowl combine 1 cup of warm water with a .25 oz. pkg. of active dry yeast and 1 tsp. of organic honey or sugar

Let stand for 5 minutes or until it is foamy

In the bowl of your mixer or food processor, add 2 ¾ c. sprouted flour and 1 tsp. salt

With the mixer running at a low speed, add the water and yeast mixture and 1 tbsp. of olive oil

Mix for 2 minutes on medium speed until a ball forms

Place in a large bowl sprayed with cooking spray

Cover bowl with plastic wrap and allow to rise for 2 hours

Roll out and it will be ready to use

2 ¾ c. sprouted flour
1 cup warm water
1 tbsp. olive oil
.25 oz. package active dry yeast
1 tsp. organic honey or sugar
1 tsp. sea salt

MEATBALLS & MARINARA

Serve with your favorite style of sprouted pasta and a large green salad for an easy, delicious family dinner

SERVES 6

1 ¼ lb. lean ground turkey, chicken or beef
1 c. bread crumbs
4 garlic cloves, minced
1 egg + 1 egg white
⅓ c. diced red onion
1 tsp. sea salt
½ tsp. black pepper
¼ c. chopped parsley
½ tsp. dried basil and
½ tsp. oregano

MEATBALLS

Method

Preheat oven to 350°F

Spray a baking sheet with non-stick spray

In a large bowl, add your choice of meat, bread crumbs, onion, garlic, parsley, basil, oregano, egg, salt and pepper

Mix well to combine and using your hands, roll into slightly larger than golf ball sized meatballs

Place on baking sheet and bake for 12–15 minutes or until cooked through

*Make your own or use organic store bought
2 tbsp. olive oil
2 large onions, diced
6 garlic cloves, minced
6 jars pureed or diced tomatoes (about 18 oz. each)
½ tsp. each of basil and oregano
2 tsp. sea salt
1 tsp. black pepper

MARINARA SAUCE

Method

Bring a large sauce pot to medium high heat and add olive oil, garlic, onions, tomatoes, basil and oregano. Sauté for a few minutes, seasoning with salt and pepper

Add 2 c. water and cook for an hour, stirring frequently, taste and add salt if needed. Cook longer to desired consistency, 2 hours max

Use right away or store and freeze

PASTA

2 c. dry pasta, cook as directed

Nutrition facts per serving: Calories 350, Carbohydrates 42g, Protein 26g, Fat 10g

Rule #7: Focus on the rules

Start small, with one or two small changes, meals cooked, gyms hit, names taken. Together, proper nutrition and exercise will get you great results and create positive habits. They will serve you well for the rest of your life.

BAKED CHICKEN TENDERS & FISH STICKS

Kids love them, you will too, add steak fries & steamed fresh green beans

SERVES 4

Method

Heat oven to 425

In shallow dish or bowl, combine flour and seasoning

In second shallow dish or bowl, combine egg (beaten) and water

In third shallow dish or bowl, combine bread crumbs and Parmesan cheese

Take each piece of chicken or fish and coat with flour, then egg mixture, then bread crumbs and cheese

Bake in oven for 15-20 minutes, turning once

Nutrition facts per serving: Calories 244, Carbohydrates 11g, Protein 31g, Fat 6g

16 oz. of chicken or white fish (like cod), cut into 2 ½ - 3" pieces
½ c. flour
1 egg
1 tbsp. water
½ c. dried bread crumbs
½ c. Parmesan cheese grated
½ tsp. garlic seasoning
½ tsp. sea salt
½ tsp. black pepper

CHILI LIME CHICKEN KABOBS

Great laid over a bed of brown rice, with grilled vegetables. Quick, easy, fun, healthy! Summer day or night favorite.

SERVES 4

4 boneless and skinless chicken breasts, cut into 1 ½" squared pieces
1 large onion, chopped into 2" squared pieces
2 bell peppers, chopped into 2" squared pieces
1 box whole or sliced mushrooms
2 c. cooked brown rice
12 long grilling skewers (soak in water for about 10 minutes before grilling)

Marinade:
4 tbsp. olive oil
2 tbsp. red wine vinegar
1 lime, juiced
3 tsp. organic taco seasoning or Mexican seasoning
Sea salt
Black pepper

Method

Place chicken in shallow baking dish along with vegetables

Make marinade, whisk together marinade ingredients and pour over chicken and vegetables

Cover and refrigerate for 1-2 hours

Preheat grill to medium high heat

Thread chicken and vegetables onto skewer, alternating 1 piece of chicken to 2 pieces of vegetables

Lightly oil grill grate

Cook for 10-15 minutes, rotating every 5 minutes or so, until chicken is done

Place over ½ c. of rice, and enjoy!

Nutrition facts per serving: Calories 379, Carbohydrates 35g, Protein 27g, Fat 14g

CEVICHE

A super easy summertime favorite...

SERVES 6

Method

Place fish in a bowl, pour lime juice over and mix to combine

Cover with lid or plastic wrap and refrigerate until fish is white throughout, about 15 minutes

Remove from refrigerator and drain lime juice, gently squeezing fish with your hands

Add tomato, onion, jalapeno, cilantro and tomato juice and season with sea salt and pepper to taste

Bake tortillas in the oven at 325 until crisp

Spoon ceviche onto tortilla and serve

Nutrition facts per serving: Calories 354, Carbohydrates 29g, Protein 41g, Fat 8g

2 lbs. sea bass, tilapia, or halibut
  cut into 1" pieces
1 c. lime juice
2 tomatoes, chopped
1 c. onion, chopped
¼ c. cilantro, chopped
½ c. tomato juice
1 jalapeno, finely diced
Salt and pepper to taste
1 avocado, thinly sliced (optional)
6 small sprouted tortillas

TACOS 2 WAYS

Any and all kinds... Shredded chicken (from Sensational slow cooked salsa chicken recipe), fish (grilled or beer battered, below), or steak (see carne asada recipe). Choose your protein and add fresh Pico de Gallo, shredded lettuce, sprouted tortillas and guacamole, ALL FROM RECIPES IN THIS BOOK! SO EASY!!!

SERVINGS: 1 LB. PROTEIN SERVES 4, 1 ½ LBS. PROTEIN SERVES 6, 2 LBS. PROTEIN SERVES 8

1 lb. cod, Mahi, haddock or halibut fillets, cut into 2-3" strips
1 pkg. small sprouted tortillas
1 tbsp. olive oil
1 c. low-fat plain yogurt
1½ limes, squeezed
3 c. shredded cabbage
½ onion, sliced
Fresh cilantro, chopped
2 tsp. Mexican seasoning
Sea salt
Black pepper

FISH TACOS

Method

Fish: In a bowl mix ½ lime squeezed, 1-2 tbsp. olive oil, 1 tsp. Mexican seasoning, ½ tsp. salt and ½ tsp. pepper

Mix and marinate in refrigerator for 15 minutes

Sauce: Mix in a small bowl 1 c. low-fat plain yogurt, ½ lime squeezed, 1 tsp. Mexican seasoning, ½ tsp. salt and ½ tsp. pepper

Slaw: Mix together 3 c. shredded cabbage, ½ onion, small handful cilantro, ½ lime squeezed, ½ tsp. salt and ½ tsp. pepper

Heat oil and cook fish in large pan over medium heat for 4-6 minutes on each side, until fish flakes. Then use pan to warm corn tortillas, keeping them warm by covering them in a clean dry dish towel until assembling tacos

Use 1 tortilla per taco, 2 tacos per person

Nutrition facts per serving: Calories 259, Carbohydrates 28g, Protein 26g, Fat 7g

BEER BATTER FISH TACOS

Method

Batter:
In a medium-sized bowl, mix and stir the following ingredients together:
1 c. sprouted flour
2 tbsp. corn starch
1 tsp. baking powder
½ tsp. sea salt
1 egg
1 c. light beer

White sauce:
In a medium-sized bowl, mix and stir the following together:
1 c. plain yogurt
½ lime juiced
1 jalapeno minced
½ tsp. each of cayenne pepper, cumin, oregano, salt, pepper

Fish:
Heat 1 qt. of oil (fill a deep pan with 1" of oil on medium high heat)

Cut 1 lb. cod fillets into 2-3" strips and dust lightly with flour

Dip strips into beer batter, fry in oil until golden brown, set on paper towel to soak up excess oil

Use 1 tortilla per taco, 2 tacos per person

Then assemble! Tortilla, fish, cabbage, Pico de Gallo, white sauce, cilantro

Nutrition facts per serving: Calories 325, Carbohydrates 28g, Protein 26g, Fat 14g

1 lb. cod fillets, cut into 2-3" strips
1 qt. oil for frying
1 pkg. small sprouted tortillas
1 c. sprouted flour
2 tbsp. corn starch
1 tsp. baking powder
½ tsp. sea salt
1 egg
1 c. light beer
1 c. low fat plain yogurt
½ lime, juiced
1 jalapeno, minced
½ tsp. each of cayenne pepper, cumin, oregano, sea salt and black pepper
3 c. shredded cabbage
Pico De Gallo
Cilantro

CARNE ASADA

Simple, easy, delicious. Try in tacos with 2 small sprouted tortillas, burritos with one large sprouted tortilla or on a salad with ½ c. black beans, and lots of Pico de Gallo and a tbsp. of fresh guacamole...

SERVES 6

2lbs flank or skirt steak

Marinade:
⅓ c. olive oil
4 cloves garlic minced
2 limes juiced
2 tbsp. white vinegar
1 tsp. cumin
1 tsp. sea salt
½ tsp. black pepper
¼ c. fresh cilantro, chopped
½ tsp. fresh orange juice, optional

Method

Mix marinade and steak in a bowl, coating steak completely

Cover bowl in plastic wrap or with a lid for 1-3 hours

Cook at medium heat on a skillet or grill, season with sea salt and black pepper

Cook for a few minutes on each side, set aside for a few more minutes to rest and slice

Warm tortillas, if desired, on the skillet and assemble!

Nutrition facts per serving: Calories 210, Carbohydrates 0g, Protein 24g, Fat 12g

BAKED WHITE FISH WITH PESTO SAUCE

Add green beans, onions and a whole grain, we use fresh baked bread from Wholefoods

SERVES 4

Pesto Sauce: Mix all pesto ingredients in a food processor and pulse until smooth

Method

Spray a large pan (with a lid) with cooking spray and heat over medium heat

Add onions and green beans and cook for 3-4 minutes, stirring occasionally

Spread onions and beans into a flat layer on the bottom, place white fish on top and sprinkle with pepper

Add chicken broth and water, place top on pan, and cook on high heat for 5-6 minutes

Using a slotted spoon, spoon beans and fish onto 4 plates

Keep broth uncovered and continue to cook at high heat, allowing it to cook and thicken for about 5-6 minutes

Remove from heat and add pesto and a squeeze of lemon juice to broth

Plate beans, onions and fish on top

Pour 2-3 tablespoons over fish, serve with a couple slices of bread

Nutrition facts per serving: Calories 409, Carbohydrates 37g, Protein 31g, Fat 16g

4 filets of white fish, cod, tilapia, turbot, etc.
2 lbs. green beans, trimmed
1 onion, sliced
1 c. chicken broth
½ c. water
⅓ c. pesto sauce (see recipe below)
1 lemon
½ tsp. black pepper
1 loaf fresh organic baked bread, sliced

Pesto Recipe:
2 c. fresh basil
3 garlic cloves, minced
⅓ c. olive oil
¼ c. pine nuts
¼ c. parmesan cheese, grated
1 tsp. sea salt
½ tsp. black pepper

WHITE FISH AND TOMATO SALSA

Seriously simple... Serve with ½ c. brown rice or fresh bread

SERVES 4

4 fillets of white fish, tilapia, cod, turbot, haddock, or halibut
(TIP: vegetarians use tempeh, eggplant or tofu)
1 large jar of your favorite organic tomato salsa
1 tbsp. olive oil
3 c. of any or a mixture of: whole mushrooms, asparagus, peppers, onions

Method

Sauté fish in a large pan on medium heat in oil until lightly browned

Pour salsa over fish and add vegetables

Turn heat to low or simmer, cover with lid and let cook for 35-40 minutes, or until vegetables are tender

Nutrition facts per serving: Calories 197, Carbohydrates 19g, Protein 21g, Fat 4g

SENSATIONAL SLOW COOKED SALSA CHICKEN

Quick, easy, healthy and tasty. This is one of the first dishes I make with kids that I work with. Serve over brown rice, with 2 small sprouted tortillas or fresh bread, with lots and lots of vegetables

SERVES 4

Method

Sauté chicken in a large pan on medium heat in oil until lightly browned

Pour salsa over chicken and add vegetables

Turn heat to low or simmer, cover with lid and let cook for 45-55 minutes

Nutrition facts per serving: Calories 204, Carbohydrates 19g, Protein 22g, Fat 4g

4 boneless, skinless chicken breasts or 6 thighs (TIP: for vegetarians use tempeh, tofu or eggplant)
1 large jar of your favorite organic salsa
1 tbsp. olive oil
3 c. any or all: whole mushrooms, asparagus, peppers, onions

SOUTH OF THE BORDER BURRITOS

Great for involving the whole family, or for parties, make buffet style with ingredients laid out and let family or guests assemble their own! They won't know how healthy they really are...

SERVES 8

24 oz. 93% ground beef or chicken (you may also use sliced cooked chicken, steak, tempeh or fish)

2 - 15 oz. cans of black or pinto beans (or one of each), or better yet, buy them dried, soak them overnight, rinse and cook in water with a pinch of sea salt

1 - 7 oz. can or jar of Mexican tomato sauce (or tomato sauce if that's all you can find)

Mozzarella cheese, shredded

1 package large sprouted tortillas

1 large onion, diced

2 large tomatoes, chopped

1 head iceberg lettuce, shredded or 1 bunch of romaine lettuce, chopped

1 tsp. sea salt

½ tsp. black pepper

½ tsp. cumin

¼ tsp. chili powder

¼ tsp. oregano

½ c. fresh cilantro, chopped

Method

Preheat oven to 180

In a large skillet over medium heat, spray with non-stick spray and cook onions for a few minutes, then add ground beef, chicken or your choice of protein until lightly browned

Add spices and salt and pepper

Add tomato sauce and stir

Lower heat to simmer and add ⅛ c. water if it gets too dry

Transfer to large dish and put other ingredients into separate dishes: beans, shredded cheese, shredded lettuce, cilantro and chopped tomatoes

Warm tortillas in pan for about 15-20 seconds on each side (optional) and serve to family for assembly

Serve with refried beans with cheese (optional)

REFRIED BEANS WITH CHEESE (OPTIONAL)

Method

In a pan on medium heat, add 1 can of cooked black or pinto beans, ½ c. water and 1 tsp. garlic powder along with one pinch of both salt and pepper

Cook for a few minutes, stirring until warmed. Using a fork, mash beans until they resemble refried beans

Add ¾ c. mozzarella to mixture and cook until lightly melted

Nutrition facts per serving: Calories 405, Carbohydrates 44g, Protein 30g, Fat 11g

1 can black or pinto beans
¾ c. shredded mozzarella cheese
½ c. water
1 tsp. garlic powder
one pinch both sea salt and black pepper

BURRITO BOWL

Similar to the South of the Border recipe, but with a nice marinade and no tortillas, you can also top a large green salad with this recipe...

SERVES 6

24 oz. skirt steak, top round or chuck roast, thinly sliced

Marinade for Carnitas:
¼ c. olive oil
4 garlic cloves, minced
1 jalapeno, chopped
1 lime or orange cut in half and juiced
2 tsp. oregano
1 tsp. cumin
1 tsp. sea salt
½ tsp. black pepper

For Burrito Bowls:
1 ½ c. cooked black beans
1 ½ c. cooked brown rice
1 large onion, chopped
2 green bell peppers, sliced
½ c. cilantro, chopped
2 c. Pico de Gallo (see recipe)
4–6 c. shredded iceberg or romaine lettuce
½ c. shredded mozzarella cheese
6 tbsp. low fat sour cream or low fat plain Greek yogurt

Method

Mix marinade and pour over beef slices, marinate beef in Ziploc bag or covered bowl in refrigerator for 1-4 hours.

Heat pan on medium/high heat and cook carnitas for a few minutes, then add sliced green peppers and chopped onions, cover and cook until done

Toss rice with cilantro, divide rice among 6 bowls

Top with beans, carnitas and cooked vegetables, then shredded lettuce, Pico de Gallo, sour cream and a sprinkle of cheese

Nutrition facts per serving: Calories 380, Carbohydrates 34g, Protein 34g, Fat 12g

CHICKEN QUESADILLAS

SERVES 4

Method

In a large skillet sauté all vegetables for 4-6 minutes on medium high heat in oil, remove from heat, add a pinch of salt and pepper

Place tortilla into skillet and flip until warm, about 10-15 seconds per side. Fill with desired ingredients, fold and let cook for a few minutes. Plate and cut into 2-4 pieces, topping with sour cream, avocado, shredded lettuce and sliced olives

Makes 2 small tortilla quesadillas per person

Nutrition facts per serving: Calories 377, Carbohydrates 37g, Protein 27g, Fat 15g

2 boneless skinless chicken breast, cooked and shredded
8 small sprouted tortillas
4 oz. shredded Monterey Jack cheese
2 bell peppers, chopped
1 large onion, chopped
1 large tomato, diced
2 garlic cloves, minced
½ c. fresh cilantro, chopped
1 tbsp. olive oil
Sea salt
Black pepper

For topping:
6 oz. low fat sour cream or plain low fat Greek yogurt
½ avocado, sliced
2 c. shredded iceberg or romaine lettuce
1 c. sliced black olives

ENCHILADAS

From my favorite Aunt Christy, for health, with love. Great for making and enjoying throughout the week, or to make for a get together.

SERVES 8

Use a 9x13 pan or casserole dish
12 small sprouted tortillas

For Sauce:
2 tbsp. olive oil
2 tsp. ground cumin
¼ c. sprouted flour
**1 7 oz. can tomato paste (small
    can – I like Muir Glen)**
1 box of vegetable or chicken broth

Filling:
12 oz. shredded mozzarella
1 can black beans
**1 package frozen spinach (thaw
    and drain/squeeze out excess
    water)**
1 package corn, thawed
2 bell peppers, chopped
2 bunches of scallions, thinly sliced
**2 boneless, skinless chicken
    breasts, cooked and shredded
    (optional)**
**2 tsp. cumin + ½ tsp. of both salt
    and pepper**

Topping:
4 oz. shredded mozzarella

Method

For Sauce:
Stir ingredients together in a pot or pan on medium heat, whisk and simmer until slightly thickened, season with ½ tsp. of both salt and pepper

Filling:
In large bowl mix all filling ingredients
Add ¾ of sauce (above) and mix together with filling

Preheat oven to 375

In 9x13 pan or casserole dish, cover bottom with ⅛th of the sauce

Layer tortillas (6) on top of spread out sauce

Add filling

Layer tortillas (6) on top of filling

Coat tortillas with last ⅛th of sauce

Sprinkle 4 oz. of shredded mozzarella cheese on top

Bake at 375 in convection oven for 45 minutes, cool, serve

Nutrition facts per serving: Calories 396, Carbohydrates 37g, Protein 24g, Fat 17g

MEXICAN RICE CASSEROLE

Ole!

SERVES 6

Method

Preheat oven to 375

In a large pan, heat oil on medium high heat

Add garlic, peppers and onions and sauté for 3-4 minutes

Reduce heat to medium heat and add rice, cooking for a couple of minutes

Add tomatoes and spices and stir, cooking for a few minutes

Add broth and chicken, stir and cook for a few more minutes

Bring contents of pan to a boil and then simmer

Stir and pour contents into an oven safe 9x13 casserole dish

Sprinkle cheese over the top and bake for 10-15 minutes

Cut and serve topped with chopped cilantro

Nutrition facts per serving: Calories 329, Carbohydrates 42g, Protein 22g, Fat 8g

1 ½ tbsp. olive oil
3 garlic cloves, minced
1 onion, chopped
2 bell peppers, chopped
3 c. brown rice, cooked
2 – 14.5 oz. cans or jars of whole tomatoes
10 oz. can of diced tomatoes with green chilies (if you can't find this, you can buy them separately, or omit the green chilies)
2 tsp. cumin
1 tsp. sea salt
½ tsp. black pepper
½ tsp. cayenne
¼ tsp. turmeric
3 boneless skinless chicken breast, cooked and chopped
Fresh cilantro, chopped
¾ c. chicken broth
¾ c. shredded Monterey jack or mozzarella cheese

BAKED FISH

Great for first time chefs, serve with brown rice or quinoa, and lightly steamed vegetables

SERVES 4

1 lb. of your favorite white fish
1 tbsp. olive oil
1 tbsp. lemon juice
½ tsp. sea salt
¼ tsp. black pepper
¼ tsp. paprika

Method

Preheat oven to 375

Spray a baking sheet with non-stick spray and place fish on sheet skin side down

Mix oil, lemon juice and spices and drizzle over fish

Bake for 15–18 minutes

Nutrition facts per serving: Calories 120, Carbohydrates 0g, Protein 20g, Fat 4g

CHRISTY'S CHICKEN BAKE

My mother and aunt's go-to recipe mid-week... Serve with steamed vegetables or large green salad

SERVES 6

Method

Set oven to convection 400 degrees

Cut up whole chicken, rinse and dry

Peel and quarter onion, potatoes, and sweet potatoes and rub vegetables and chicken lightly with olive oil

Place all on baking sheet sprayed with non-stick spray and lightly season with salt, pepper and garlic seasoning

Add ¼ c. white wine and ¼ c. water to bottom of cookie sheet

Cook for 15 minutes uncovered, then cover with foil for 20-25 minutes, uncover and bake another 15 minutes until brown

Nutrition facts per serving: Calories 373, Carbohydrates 25g, Protein 32g, Fat 16g

1 whole chicken, cut up
3 medium potatoes
3 medium sweet potatoes
1 onion
¼ c. white wine or use chicken broth if white wine is not available
Olive oil
Sea salt
Black pepper
Herb – garlic seasoning

GS! ROSEMARY CHICKEN

Bake it with quartered potatoes and asparagus, dinner is served in 30 minutes

SERVES 4

8 boneless and skinless chicken
    thighs
4 medium potatoes, cut into
    quarters
1 large bunch asparagus
¼ c. olive oil
1 ½ tbsp. rosemary
2 tsp. oregano
2 tsp. garlic powder
1 tsp. sea salt
½ tsp. black pepper

Method

Preheat oven to 350

In a large bowl, place chicken, potatoes and asparagus

Using your hands, lightly rub oil over everything, sprinkle with herbs, salt and pepper

Mix it all together until everything has a light coating of oil

Place on a baking sheet and bake for 30-35 minutes

Nutrition facts per serving: Calories 346, Carbohydrates 22g, Protein 31g, Fat 16g

LEMON HERB CHICKEN

Enjoy with ½ c. whole grain pasta or brown rice and steamed vegetables

SERVES 4

Method

Place flour in a shallow dish, moisten chicken breasts slightly with water and coat with flour

In a large skillet or pan, sauté garlic in oil for a couple minutes on medium high heat

Add chicken to skillet, cooking for 3–4 minutes each side until brown, season with salt, pepper and herbs

Remove chicken from pan and add broth, lemon juice and 1 tbsp. flour, whisk together and bring to a boil stirring frequently

Cook for about 5–6 minutes or until slightly thickened, return chicken to pan and cook for a few minutes

Nutrition facts per serving: Calories 234, Carbohydrates 8g, Protein 28g, Fat 10g

- 1 lb. chicken breast, sliced in half lengthwise
- 2 tbsp. olive oil
- 5 garlic cloves, minced
- ¼ c. sprouted flour
- 1 c. chicken broth
- 1 tbsp. fresh squeezed lemon juice
- 1 ½ tsp. fresh or dried oregano
- 1 tsp. fresh or dried thyme minced
- 1 tsp. sea salt
- ½ tsp. black pepper

GRASS FED BEEF OR BISON CHILI

With Spicy Cornbread

SERVES 4

½ tbsp. olive oil
1 lb. ground beef or bison
1 large onion, chopped
4 large carrots, chopped
1 head cauliflower, chopped
    (about 3 c.)
2 bell peppers, diced
4 garlic cloves, minced
3 tsp. cumin
2 tbsp. chili powder
1 - 28 oz. can/jar crushed tomatoes
1 – 15 oz. can/jar diced tomatoes
1 – 15 oz. can kidney beans,
    drained and rinsed
1 jalapeno diced
Fresh cilantro, chopped
1 tbsp. apple cider vinegar
Salt and pepper to taste

Method

Add oil to large stew pot. Over medium heat, cook beef/bison for 5 minutes

Add garlic, onions, jalapeno and carrots, cook for 5 minutes

Add ½ c. water

Add bell peppers and cauliflower, cook for 5 minutes

Add cumin and chili powder, vinegar, tomatoes, beans and 1 c. water

Bring to a boil then reduce to simmer, cover and cook stirring occasionally for about 45 minutes

Serve with chopped cilantro and add salt and pepper to taste

Nutrition facts per serving: Calories 284, Carbohydrates 24g, Protein 29g, Fat 8g

How are we doing? Getting frustrated? Step back a bit. Not getting results? Check your program and food/activity log. The answers lie within…

Getting amazing results? You're welcome.

Either way, I know your potential and am proud of you. Be proud of yourself for picking up this book and making a decision to Get Skinny! You have taken the first necessary step towards true health.

It works. Trust, Believe, Commit, it's a lifestyle, it gets easier and you get better. Practice and planning makes perfect. It's a beautiful thing. Trust me.

JIM'S CHICKEN CHILI

This is my dad's special recipe, it's a healthy crowd-pleaser

SERVES 6

1 lb. boneless, skinless chicken breast or thighs, cooked and chopped
1 - 28 oz. can or jar of diced tomatoes
1 tbsp. olive oil
2 cloves garlic, minced
1 onion chopped
2 green peppers, chopped
1 - 12 oz. can corn kernels, or 2 ears fresh corn
1 - 7 oz. can diced green chilies
1 - 16 oz. can beans (ranch style with jalapenos if possible)
1 - 16 oz. can black or pinto beans
1 tsp. each of cumin and chili pepper
2 c. chicken broth
1 jalapeno, diced
½ c. fresh cilantro, chopped
Sea salt and black pepper to taste

Toppings:
1 lime, juiced
1 tbsp. plain low fat Greek yogurt (optional)
Light sprinkle shredded mozzarella (optional)
½ serving sprouted tortilla chips (optional)
salt and pepper to taste

Method

In a large 8 qt. kettle, heat oil, then add onion and peppers, cooking for 4-5 minutes

Add all ingredients (except for chicken and cilantro), heat to a boil and simmer for 10 minutes

Add chicken and simmer 10 more minutes

Remove from heat and stir in cilantro

Plate and squeeze a little lime juice over each bowl, add a few tortilla chips, sprinkle some cheese over it all and add a dollop of Greek yogurt, if desired

Nutrition facts per serving: Calories 380, Carbohydrates 27g, Protein 30g, Fat 11g
(With all optional ingredients)

OVEN FRIED CHICKEN

The healthy way to enjoy fried chicken, I usually make this with baked sweet potatoes and steamed fresh green beans

SERVES 4

Method

Preheat oven to 350

Spray a baking sheet or cover in foil

Combine crackers, spices, and parmesan in a shallow bowl

In a large bowl, combine eggs, yogurt, and mustard

Dip chicken into the yogurt mixture and then into the cracker mix

Bake for 45 minutes

Nutrition facts per serving: Calories 325, Carbohydrates 21g, Protein 37g, Fat 10g

- 4 boneless, skinless chicken breasts, or 6 thighs (it is ok if you want to use chicken with the skin on)
- 3 servings of organic crackers (about 40 crackers), or try organic corn flakes cereal – 1 ¼ c. total when pulsed, processed, blended or crushed. (I use Mary's Gone Crackers, herb flavor or black pepper, pulsed in a food processor, crushed with a knife handle, or I put them in a bag and crush them with a rolling pin.)
- 2 tbsp. parmesan cheese
- ½ c. plain low fat yogurt
- 2 eggs
- 1 tsp. cayenne pepper
- ½ tsp. garlic powder
- 1 tbsp. Dijon mustard (regular is ok too)
- ½ tsp. of both sea salt and black pepper

CHICKEN MARSALA

Serve with brown rice and steamed broccoli

SERVES 4

4 chicken breasts, cut in half and/or
    pounded flat (about ¼" thick)
⅓ c. sprouted flour
1 tsp. sea salt
½ tsp. pepper
1 ½ tsp. oregano
2 tbsp. butter
2 boxes mushrooms, sliced
¾ c. sweet Marsala wine

Method

In shallow dish or bowl, mix flour, salt, pepper and oregano, then coat chicken pieces

In large skillet with lid, melt butter over medium heat. Place chicken in pan, lightly brown, then turn. Add mushrooms and Marsala wine. Cover with lid and cook for 10 minutes, turning chicken once.

Nutrition facts per serving: Calories 279, Carbohydrates 19g, Protein 26g, Fat 6g

CHICKEN CACCIATORE

Impress your friends, and their waistlines...

SERVES 4

Method

In a large pan or skillet, heat 1 tbsp. olive oil on medium heat and add garlic, onions, and peppers. Cook for 5 minutes, stirring occasionally

Add mushrooms and tomato paste, cook for a few more minutes

Add chicken broth and tomatoes, continue to stir

Bring to a boil and then simmer for 5 minutes

Add salt and pepper, oregano and thyme, chicken and juices from the plate

Simmer for 5 more minutes, then stir in basil leaves

Nutrition facts per serving: Calories 279, Carbohydrates 21g, Protein 24g, Fat 6g

4 cooked chicken breasts or thighs (With skin on, if desired, season with sea salt and black pepper, bake at 375 skin side down for 20 minutes, turning after 10 minutes.)
1 tbsp. olive oil
1 onion, diced
2 bell pepper, diced
1 box mushrooms, sliced
4 cloves garlic, minced
4 c. plum tomatoes, diced
2 hot cherry peppers
1 c. chicken broth
¼ c. tomato paste
½ c. fresh basil
1 tsp. fresh or dried thyme and oregano
1 ½ tsp. sea salt
¾ tsp. black pepper

HEALTHY MAC N CHEESE

A family favorite, I'll do anything to get those vegetables in...

SERVES 8

2 bags frozen or fresh vegetables: Anything that you like, I use frozen vegetable medley of carrots, broccoli, cauliflower, or 1 bag frozen spinach (thawed and excess water squeezed out), fresh sliced mushrooms and onions, and sometimes I will add diced tomatoes too (really good)! Be creative, just get those veggies in...

12 oz. your favorite macaroni, I use Jovial from Italy

16 oz. shredded cheese – Mozzarella (recommended), sharp cheddar, Monterey jack, Italian blend, or pepper jack

1 c. low fat milk

1 large chicken breast, shredded (optional)

Regular or Dijon Mustard

Sea salt and black pepper

Method

Preheat oven to 350

Cook macaroni as directed

Mix hot macaroni, cheese, and vegetables. Then add 1 c. low fat milk, and 1-2 tsp. of regular or Dijon mustard, and salt and pepper

Add chicken (optional)

Bake 30 minutes at 350

Nutrition facts per serving: Calories 355, Carbohydrates 34g, Protein 25g, Fat 12g

BAKED ZITI

As with many of our dishes, this is a great one to make and eat or to make and freeze. Lots of nutrients, vegetables, protein and fiber. You may use gluten free pasta if desired.

SERVES 8

Method

Make pasta according to package

Mix ricotta or low-fat cottage cheese with the thawed and drained spinach

Preheat oven to 350

Spray a large pan with cooking spray and place over medium high heat

Add garlic and let cook for a minute or two before adding meat

Cook until about halfway done, then add ½ tsp. each of sea salt and black pepper, 1 tbsp. Italian seasoning and 1 tbsp. basil or rosemary

Add onions, peppers and mushrooms to pan cook for 3-4 more minutes and then add marinara sauce

In a 9x13 baking dish spread a layer of pasta (about half of the pasta), then a layer of the meat sauce and vegetables, then a layer of spinach ricotta or low fat cottage cheese, then another layer of pasta (the other half), followed by the rest of the meat sauce and vegetables. Top with a sprinkling of mozzarella cheese followed by parmesan cheese

Bake in oven for 20 minutes

1 lb. pasta
1 lb. lean ground beef, chopped chicken, ground turkey, tempeh or go vegetarian!
1 large jar of marinara sauce
3-4 garlic cloves, minced
½ onion, chopped
1 c. sliced mushrooms
1 large bell pepper, chopped
1 c. frozen spinach, thawed and drained
1 c. ricotta or low-fat cottage cheese
½ c. mozzarella, shredded
¼ c. parmesan cheese, grated
1 tbsp. rosemary or basil
1 tbsp. Italian seasoning
½ tsp. red pepper flakes
½ tsp. sea salt
½ tsp. black pepper

Nutrition facts per serving: Calories 433, Carbohydrates 43g, Protein 27g, Fat 10g

(with 93/7% grass fed beef)

PERFECT TOP SIRLOIN

Serve with red potatoes, green beans and a salad

SERVES 4

Method

Heat a grill, griddle or frying pan to high heat

Lightly brush steak with olive oil and season with salt and pepper

TIP: Only grill one steak at a time, if you try for more, it will skew the temperature

Once grill is smoking hot, cook steak for 2–3 minutes per side

Remove steak from heat and let rest for 4–5 minutes before serving

Nutrition facts per serving: Calories 195, Carbohydrates 0g, Protein 31g, Fat 8g

1 lb. top sirloin steak
1 tbsp. olive oil
1 tsp. sea salt
½ tsp. black pepper

PAINLESS POT ROAST

A great recipe to prepare and leave to itself to finish while you tend to other matters. I like to make mine and then add a green vegetable, such as easily steamed green beans or a nice salad to bring balance to the meal.

SERVES 4

24 oz. beef chuck roast
2 onions, sliced
1 bag carrots, chopped (about 1 lb.)
2 potatoes, cut and quartered
1 box beef stock
Fresh or dried rosemary and thyme, about 1 tsp. each (to be added to liquid)
1 box mushrooms
4 garlic cloves, chopped
1 tbsp. olive oil
½ c. red wine (optional but recommended)
Sea salt
Black pepper

Method

Preheat oven to 275

Heat a large pan that has a lid on medium high heat. Once hot, add olive oil

Lightly salt and pepper roast, making sure that all sides are coated

Place meat into pan and brown on all sides, about 2-3 minutes per side, then pull out

Add all vegetables, except mushrooms but including garlic, to the pan and brown them in the meat's juices for a few minutes

Add meat back to pan and add broth, mushrooms, rosemary and thyme. Bake for 3 hours

Pull out and let cool for 10 minutes and plate

Nutrition facts per serving: Calories 379, Carbohydrates 32g, Protein 36g, Fat 9g

STIR FRY

Simple, easy, healthy, delicious! Add ½ c. brown rice or quinoa for a balanced meal

SERVES 4

Tip: Feel free to exchange any vegetables out for some of your favorites, mushrooms, green onions, etc.

Method

Start by cutting up all meat and vegetables, once you start, it goes quick…

In a large wok or skillet heat oil on medium heat and add fish or chicken, cooking for 3-4 minutes until done, stir constantly

Stirring constantly, add peppers and onions and cook for 1-2 minutes

Add squash, broccoli and eggplant, cook for 1-2 minutes, stirring constantly

Add garlic and teriyaki sauce, keep stirring, cook for 1-2 minutes

Add bok choy, sprouts, snow peas, salt and pepper, then cook and stir for 2-4 minutes until done

Nutrition facts per serving: Calories 281, Carbohydrates 20g, Protein 25g, Fat 10g

1 lb. of fish or chicken, sliced into 1 ½" pieces
2 ½ tbsp. sesame oil
2 bell peppers (one red, one yellow if possible), sliced
½ red onion, sliced
1 c. yellow squash, sliced
1 c. broccoli florets
1 baby eggplant, chopped
1 c. baby bok choy, chopped
1 c. fresh mung bean sprouts
½ c. snow peas
½ c. teriyaki sauce
1 garlic clove, minced
1 tsp. black pepper
1 tsp. sea salt

CHINESE CHICKEN AND MUSHROOMS

SERVES 4

4 boneless, skinless chicken
   breasts or thighs, cut into 1 ½"
   pieces
¾ c. oyster sauce
2 tbsp. corn starch
2 tbsp. organic sesame oil
6 scallions, chopped into 1" pieces
2" Fresh ginger, thinly sliced
4 garlic cloves, minced
1 large box mushrooms, sliced
16 oz. baby bok choy, cut into 1 ½"
   pieces
1 ¼ c. chicken broth
2 c. brown rice, cooked

Method

Toss the chicken pieces with the oyster sauce in a bowl

In another bowl mix corn starch with 3 tbsp. water

Heat wok or large pan over high heat until pan or wok is hot

Add oil, garlic, ginger and scallions and stir fry for 30 seconds

Add chicken and stir fry for 2-3 minutes, then stir in mushrooms, bok choy, and broth and bring to a full boil

Add corn starch mixture and bring to a full boil again

Cook for 3-4 minutes

Serve over rice

Nutrition facts per serving: Calories 350, Carbohydrates 28g, Protein 30g, Fat 13g

BEEF AND BROCCOLI

Chinese made easy... and healthy!

SERVES 4

Method

Combine 2 tbsp. cornstarch and 2 tbsp. water with garlic powder and mix together

Add beef and coat

Add oil to a large skillet over medium heat, stir fry beef until cooked medium rare (brown on the outside and still red in the middle), then remove

Add broccoli and onion to pan and stir fry for 4-5 minutes then return beef to pan

In a separate bowl, mix soy sauce, ginger, 1 tbsp. corn starch, ½ c. water and sugar together then add to skillet

Cook and stir for 2 min, serve over rice

Nutrition facts per serving: Calories 361, Carbohydrates 32g, Protein 32g, Fat 12g

1 lb. round steak, cut into 3" strips
6 c. broccoli florets
3 tbsp. corn starch
½ c. water
2 tbsp. water divided
½ tsp. garlic powder
2 tbsp. olive oil
1 onion cut into wedges
¼ c. soy sauce
1 tbsp. brown sugar
1 tsp. ground ginger
2 c. cooked brown rice

TERIYAKI SALMON OR CHICKEN

Great taste and amazing flavor, enjoy with brown rice and steamed vegetables...

SERVES 4

4 – 4 oz. salmon fillets or chicken breasts/thighs
2 tbsp. sesame oil
1 lemon, juiced
¼ c. soy sauce
2 tbsp. brown sugar
1 tbsp. sesame seeds (optional)
4 green onions, sliced
1 tsp. ground mustard
1 tsp. ginger
½ tsp. garlic powder

Method

Preheat oven to 350

Place salmon or chicken aside in a casserole dish

Mix all other ingredients except salmon and simmer on low for 5–10 minutes

Pour over salmon and cover dish, refrigerate

Marinate salmon for 30 minutes to 2 hours, if time permits

Place salmon or chicken on a baking sheet covered with foil

Bake for 14–18 minutes for salmon, or 20-24 minutes for chicken

Enjoy with 2 c. brown rice divided into 4 servings and steamed vegetables

Nutrition facts per serving: Calories 389, Carbohydrates 41g, Protein 28g, Fat 12g

TERIYAKI CHICKEN & SALMON RICE BOWLS

Why buy takeout? Make your own! It will be fresher, healthier, and tastier...

SERVES 4

Method

Pour 1 tbsp. sesame oil into pan and sauté chicken or salmon for 4–6 minutes on medium high heat, until done, remove to plate

Pour 1 tbsp. sesame oil into pan and sauté vegetables and green onions for 4-6 minutes

Mix teriyaki sauce into vegetables

Plate the rice, add vegetables, then your chopped chicken or salmon

Nutrition facts per serving: Calories 389, Carbohydrates 41g, Protein 28g, Fat 12g

- 2 c. cooked brown rice
- 4 - 4 oz. chicken breasts, thighs or salmon fillets, cut into 2" pieces
- 6 c. chopped vegetables (carrots, broccoli, zucchini, celery, red onion, cabbage)
- 2 tbsp. sesame or olive oil
- ¾ c. teriyaki sauce
- 1 bunch green onions, chopped

FAJITAS

Mahi, Chicken, Steak, Tempeh, Eggplant, Portabella Mushroom, be creative with your protein source or what you are using in place of it, and try new things...

SERVES 6

4 - 6 oz. pieces of your choice of protein, thinly sliced into approximately 2" pieces
4 garlic cloves, minced
2 zucchini, sliced
1 box of mushrooms, sliced
1 onion, chopped
2 bell peppers, chopped
2 tbsp. of a good medium high heat oil, sunflower or grapeseed for example
1 bunch cilantro, chopped
1 c. shredded mozzarella cheese
1 can or 1 c. dried black beans – soak overnight then rinse and cook, add a pinch of salt and pepper
8 small sprouted corn or flour tortillas
4 tsp. fajita seasoning
1 tsp. sea salt
½ tsp. black pepper
Pico De Gallo (see recipe, optional)

Method

Sauté garlic in 1 tbsp. of oil on medium high heat for 1-2 minutes, then add your choice of protein

Cook your protein for 4-5 minutes on each side, or until done. Season with salt, pepper and 2 tsp. fajita seasoning and remove to a plate

Add another tbsp. of oil to the pan, add vegetables, sauté for 4-5 minutes. Season with salt, pepper and 2 tsp. fajita seasoning, and remove to a plate

Finally, toss tortillas one at a time into pan for 30 seconds each side. Plate and wrap them in a dish towel to keep warm

Plate your protein, vegetables, and beans on a large dish and sprinkle with cheese and chopped cilantro

Nutrition facts per serving: Calories 369, Carbohydrates 32g, Protein 31g, Fat 12g

THAI CHICKEN SATAY

With Brown Rice and Steamed Broccoli

SERVES 5

Method

Stir together marinade, mix with chicken in a bowl and marinate for 2 hours. Cook on a grill or in a pan on medium high heat for about 4-5 minutes per side

Combine all ingredients (except lime juice and soy sauce) for satay into a saucepan. Simmer over medium high heat for 10-15 minutes until thickened (stir constantly)

Remove from heat and stir in lime juice and soy sauce

Pour over brown rice, steamed broccoli and chicken, enjoy!

Nutrition facts per serving: Calories 348, Carbohydrates 26g, Protein 28g, Fat 16g

Marinade:
1 c. light coconut milk
2 clove minced garlic
2 tsp. curry powder
3 tsp. brown sugar
1 tsp. salt
1 tsp. pepper
4 chicken breasts cut into 1" strips

Satay sauce:
1 c. light coconut milk
1 tbsp. curry powder
⅓ c. creamy peanut or almond butter
¾ c. chicken broth
¼ c. brown sugar
2 tbsp. lime juice
1 tsp. soy sauce (or 1 packet)

VEGETABLE FRIED RICE

Chinese the GS! way! So easy, so good...

SERVES 6

1 tbsp. sesame oil
3 c. cooked brown rice
3 eggs + 3 egg whites
4-5 garlic cloves, diced
2" fresh ginger, sliced
½ c. carrots, chopped
2 bell peppers, sliced
6 scallions chopped
1 c. frozen peas
1 ½ c. sliced mushrooms
½ c. onion, diced
½ c. cashews
⅓ c. tamari sauce, add more to
    taste if needed
1 large cooked chicken breast
    boneless and skinless, diced

Method

Heat a large wok or pan on medium high heat and add oil

Add eggs and cook with garlic and ginger until halfway done

Add carrots, pepper, onions, mushrooms and nuts, cook for 5 minutes

Add rice, peas, chicken and tamari sauce, cook for 5-7 minutes

Serve!

Nutrition facts per serving: Calories 249, Carbohydrates 34g, Protein 17g, Fat 6g

LO MEIN

Healthy Chinese, continued...

SERVES 6

Method

Heat a large pan or wok on high heat, when hot add oil, then immediately add peas, mushrooms, scallions, peppers and sprouts, stir fry for 1-2 minutes

Add ginger and garlic and stir fry for 2-3 minutes

Add noodles and toss to combine

Add tamari and toss cooking for 2-3 minutes

Add chicken, tossing again and then serve

Nutrition facts per serving: Calories 343, Carbohydrates 48g, Protein 20g, Fat 7g

12 oz. angel hair whole grain pasta cooked as directed on package
1 8 oz. cooked chicken breast boneless and skinless, chopped
2" ginger minced
4-5 cloves garlic minced
2 c. bean sprouts
2 red bell pepper chopped
2 tbsp. sesame oil
1 ½ c. snow peas (regular frozen peas are fine too)
2 c. sliced mushrooms
6 scallions sliced
½ c. tamari

SIDES

Rule #8: Step it up

You are now serving high quality meals that would punch America's restaurant quality food in the face!

Own it. Personalize your meals to your own likes or dislikes. Start making larger batches and freezing some or all of it to have meals later in the next few weeks, for a quick healthy meal reheated in the oven.

COLESLAW

Great for summer BBQ's and family picnics! Goes great with oven fried chicken...

SERVES 6

Method

Whisk together mayonnaise, yogurt, honey, vinegar, celery seeds, salt and pepper in a large bowl

Add cabbage and carrots, tossing to combine

Cover and refrigerate

Nutrition facts per serving: Calories 79, Carbohydrates 11g, Protein 2g, Fat 5g

⅓ c. low fat mayonnaise or light veganaise

2 tbsp. plain low-fat Greek yogurt

1 ½ tbsp. apple cider vinegar

2 tsp. raw honey

1 tsp. celery seeds (optional)

1 tsp. sea salt

½ tsp. black pepper

4 c. green cabbage, thinly sliced

4 c. red cabbage, thinly sliced

3 medium sized carrots, grated

STEAMED VEGETABLES

SERVES 4

4-6 c. of one or a variety of
    vegetables: broccoli,
    asparagus, green beans, be
    creative!
1 tsp. sea salt
½ tsp. black paper

Method

1 If you have a steaming pot, fill bottom pot with an inch or two of water, then place top pot (the one with holes in the bottom), inside and fill with vegetables and cover with lid

    Continue to #3

2 If you do not have a steaming pot, you may use this method, just stir more frequently if you do not. A large pot or pan or wok will work fine

    Continue to #3

3 Bring an inch or two of water to a simmer

    You'll have to make slight adjustments based on the size and density of your vegetables, but this is the basic idea and best way to learn, PRACTICE!

    Cook them until they're bright, and just tender

    You may finish with a light drizzle (1 tbsp.) olive oil (optional), and a sprinkle of salt and pepper

Nutrition facts per serving: Calories 83, Carbohydrates 9g, Protein 2g, Fat 0g

Nutrition facts are without olive oil

SAUTÉED VEGETABLES

SERVES 4

Method

In a large pan over medium high heat, heat oil and add garlic, sautéing for 1 minute

Add all vegetables to the pan, cooking for a few minutes, vegetables should start to wilt

Add salt, pepper and Italian seasoning, if desired

Cook for 3–4 more minutes

Serve

Nutrition facts per serving: Calories 83, Carbohydrates 11g, Protein 3g, Fat 2g

4-5 c. chopped vegetables
You may use: yellow squash, spinach, eggplant, broccoli, zucchini, thickly sliced mushrooms, bell peppers, onions, asparagus, etc.
1 tbsp. olive oil
¼ c. chicken broth
2 garlic cloves, minced
1 tsp. sea salt
½ tsp. black pepper
½ tsp. Italian seasoning (optional)

GRILLED VEGETABLES

SERVES 10

6–8 vegetables, or cups of chopped
vegetables
You may use: Yellow squash,
eggplant, zucchini, whole
mushrooms, bell peppers,
onions, asparagus, green
onions, etc.
3 tbsp. olive oil or olive oil spray
1 ½ tbsp. balsamic vinegar
3 garlic cloves, minced
1 tsp. Italian seasoning
1 tsp. sea salt
½ tsp. black pepper

Method

Using a barbecue or a grill pan, lightly brush the vegetables
with 2 tbsp. of olive oil (or light spray) and sprinkle with salt
and pepper

Grill vegetables until tender and slightly charred, different
vegetables take different times to cook

Whisk 1 tbsp. olive oil together with vinegar, Italian
seasoning, garlic and a dash of salt and pepper in a small
bowl and drizzle over vegetables

**Nutrition facts per serving: Calories 50, Carbohydrates
3g, Protein 1g, Fat 3.5g**

BEANS AND GREENS

SERVES 6

Method

Using a large skillet, heat olive oil over medium heat and sauté garlic and onions for a couple minutes

Add beans and greens and stir until lightly cooked

Add broth and simmer for a few minutes

Sprinkle with salt and pepper

Nutrition facts per serving: Calories 93, Carbohydrates 13g, Protein 5g, Fat 3g

6 c. fresh or frozen spinach (if frozen, thaw and drain excess water)

TIP: you can use any cruciferous vegetable, kale, collard greens, escarole…

1 can cannellini beans

1 onion, chopped

2 c. chicken broth

1 tbsp. olive oil

4 garlic cloves, minced

1 tsp. sea salt

½ tsp. black pepper

ROASTED BRUSSELS SPROUTS

Great with chicken or steak, rice and/or potatoes, and of course a large salad ☺

SERVES 6

1 ½ lbs. Brussels sprouts
1 ½ tbsp. olive oil
1 tsp. sea salt
½ tsp. black pepper

Method

Preheat oven to 400

Mix all in a large bowl

Place Brussels sprouts on baking sheet and bake for 35-40 minutes

Nutrition facts per serving: Calories 62, Carbohydrates 6g, Protein 3g, Fat 3g

ROASTED CAULIFLOWER

SERVES 6

Method

Preheat oven to 450

In a bowl toss together all ingredients and lay out on a baking sheet

Roast in oven for 20 minutes

Nutrition facts per serving: Calories 75, Carbohydrates 8g, Protein 3g, Fat 5g

1 large head cauliflower, cut into florets
2 tbsp. olive oil
4 garlic cloves, chopped
2 tsp. sea salt
½ tsp. black pepper

MACARONI SALAD

Outdoor party or picnic, this is a winner!

SERVES 6

4 c. whole grain pasta, cooked
½ c. low fat mayonnaise
½ c. low fat plain yogurt
¼ c. apple cider vinegar
1 large white onion, diced
3 celery stalks, chopped
1 green pepper, chopped
2-3 large carrots, sliced
1 tsp. organic sugar
2 ½ tsp. mustard
1 ½ tsp. sea salt
½ tsp. black pepper

Method

Mix together pasta, mayonnaise, yogurt, vinegar, sugar, mustard, salt and pepper

Add in vegetables and mix together

Refrigerate to let the flavor set in

Nutrition facts per serving: Calories 147, Carbohydrates 25g, Protein 4g, Fat 4g

POTATO SALAD

Method

Fill a large pot about halfway full of water and add a few dashes of sea salt

Bring water to a boil and add potatoes

Cook for about 12-15 minutes until tender but still firm, drain and allow to cool

In a large bowl combine all ingredients except potatoes, celery and onion, saving them to add last

Add potatoes, celery and onions and toss gently

Served chilled or at room temperature

Nutrition facts per serving: Calories 165, Carbohydrates 29g, Protein 4g, Fat 5g

2 lbs. red or white potatoes, cut and quartered
⅓ c. light mayonnaise
½ c. plain low fat Greek yogurt
2 tbsp. mustard, Dijon or whole grain stoneground is best
1 c. celery, sliced
½ c. red, white or yellow onion, chopped
2 tsp. sea salt
1 tsp. black pepper
1 tsp. sugar

QUINOA AND BLACK BEAN SALAD

Sensationally healthy, super easy... I like to add this to a large green salad and add some sliced chicken or steak on top. A great healthy balanced meal.

SERVES 6

1 c. cooked quinoa
½ red onion, chopped
1 – 15 oz. can black beans, drained and rinsed
1 c. fresh or frozen (defrosted) corn
3 medium tomatoes, diced
1 tbsp. olive oil
¼ c. cilantro, chopped
1 lime, juiced
½ tsp. sea salt
1 dash of black pepper
1 jalapeno, diced (optional)

Method

Mix all together in a large bowl, and serve

Nutrition facts per serving: Calories 144, Carbohydrates 25g, Protein 7g, Fat 3g

ROASTED POTATOES AND/ OR STEAK FRIES

It all depends on how you cut them, in quarters or as steak fries. Try seasoning with rosemary or garlic powder or other like herbs...

SERVES 6

Method

Preheat oven to 450

Wash, cut and quarter potatoes, then dry them

Rub with olive oil

Season with salt and pepper

Place on baking sheet and bake for 40-45 minutes

Nutrition facts per serving: Calories 141, Carbohydrates 25g, Protein 2g, Fat 5g

2 lbs. Yukon potatoes
2 tbsp. olive oil
1 tsp. sea salt
½ tsp. black pepper

MASHED POTATOES

SERVES 6

2 lbs. Yukon potatoes
1 c. 2% milk
2 tbsp. butter
1 tsp. sea salt
½ tsp. black pepper

Method

Fill a large pot about halfway full of water and add a few dashes of sea salt

Bring water to a boil and add potatoes

Cook for about 15 minutes until tender but still firm

Drain water and add butter, milk, salt and pepper

Using a potato masher, mash ingredients together until smooth

Nutrition facts per serving: Calories 156, Carbohydrates 27g, Protein 3g, Fat 5g

TURKEY DRESSING

Use vegetable broth instead of chicken broth for vegetarians...

SERVES 12

Method

Preheat oven to 250°F

Spray a 9X13" baking dish with non-stick spray

Place bread in a single layer on a baking sheet

Bake until bread is dried out, about 45 minutes. Let cool and transfer to a large bowl

Melt butter in a large skillet over medium-high heat

Add onions and celery and stir until just beginning to brown then add to the bowl with bread

Stir in herbs, salt, and pepper

Drizzle in 1 ½ c. broth and toss

Preheat oven to 350°F. Whisk ½ c. broth, ½ c. water and eggs in a bowl

Add to bread mixture and mix gently until thoroughly combined, then spoon into 9x13" baking dish and cover with foil

Bake for 30–35 minutes, remove foil and bake for 10–15 minutes more until top is crisp

Nutrition facts per serving: Calories 144, Carbohydrates 19g, Protein 3g, Fat 6g

¼ c. unsalted butter
16 oz. day-old French or sprouted
    grain bread, torn into 1" pieces
2 large eggs
2 c. chicken broth, divided
    (or vegetable broth for
    vegetarian)
2 large yellow onions, chopped
6 celery stalks, sliced
½ c. flat-leaf parsley, chopped
2 tbsp. fresh sage, chopped
1 tbsp. fresh rosemary, chopped
1 tbsp. fresh thyme, chopped
2 tsp. sea salt
1 tsp. black pepper
½ c. water

SWEET POTATO CASSEROLE

SERVES 6

2 large sweet potatoes, cubed
2 eggs, beaten
¼ c. brown sugar
½ c. 2% Milk
2 tbsp. butter, softened
½ tsp. salt
½ tsp. vanilla
⅓ c. pecans, chopped

Method

Preheat oven to 325

Place sweet potatoes in a medium pan and cover with water, cook on medium high heat until tender, drain and mash (or you can bake them in the oven at 350 until soft, about 35–45 minutes, cut in half and scoop out)

In a large bowl mix together all ingredients, saving pecans until the rest is mixed until smooth

Spoon contents into a 9x13" baking dish

Bake for 25-30 minutes

Nutrition facts per serving: Calories 187, Carbohydrates 30g, Protein 4g, Fat 6g

BISCUITS

SERVES 12

Method

Preheat oven to 450

In a large bowl combine ingredients, mix well until the dough comes together, it will be sticky

Dust hands with flour and take out about a 1 inch (large tablespoon sized) piece and roll into a ball

Place onto a baking sheet sprayed with non-stick spray

Bake for 15-20 minutes, until tall and golden on top

Nutrition facts per serving: Calories 76, Carbohydrates 9g, Protein 3g, Fat 3g

2 c. sprouted flour
1 c. buttermilk
2 tbsp. butter, softened
4 tsp. baking powder
¼ tsp. baking soda
¾ tsp. sea salt

CORNBREAD

¼ c. butter, softened
3 tbsp. honey
¼ c. applesauce
2 eggs
1 c. 2% milk
½ tsp. baking soda
1 c. cornmeal
1 c. sprouted flour
¼ c. frozen corn
1 jalapeno, finely chopped
    (optional)
½ tsp. salt

Method

Preheat oven to 375

Spray an 8" pan with non-stick spray

Mix ingredients together in a large bowl and pour into pan

Bake for 30–35 minutes or until inserted toothpick comes out clean

Nutrition facts per serving: Calories 178, Carbohydrates 24g, Protein 5g, Fat 7g

DESSERTS

Desserts are a tough call. For some of my clients, it is hard to have them around. They either eat too much or have them too often. The problem today is that our foods, desserts especially, are far too stimulating and make us only want more. My Chocolate Cake (below), for example, got a lot of scrutiny from my professional chefs for not being chocolaty enough or sweet enough. This recipe is perfect and I challenge you to get your taste buds back to where they should be. I have a piece of this cake or one cupcake and it fulfills and satisfies as a treat without making me want more. This is how food was meant to be. Do you really think Adam and Eve had fruit eating contests? Or gorged themselves on apples and bananas? Remember, *Getting Skinny! The Organic Way* is not just a new look, it's a new feeling. This is the way to look and feel great, without feeling like you are missing out on something. Take a good look at all the things that make you want more of them. Most of them are keeping you from where you want to, and need to be.

"Change your mind to change your body, change your body to change your mind."
-Andrew

Rule #9: Don't make dessert a habit.

Once or twice a week have something, it's a special reward for staying on target.

CREAMY NUT BUTTER DIP

Use celery or fruit slices for dipping, or just eat with a spoon...

SERVES 3

Method

Mix together in a bowl, with a spoon, or in a mixer

Nutrition facts per serving: Calories 83, Carbohydrates 7g, Protein 7g, Fat 4g

6 oz. plain Greek low-fat yogurt
1 tbsp. your favorite nut butter or
   2 tbsp. organic peanut butter powder
½ tbsp. maple syrup or honey
1-2 tsp. cinnamon

POWER PUDDING

Great for my athletes as a nighttime treat, snack, or after a workout! Try adding bananas, fruit or nuts...

SERVES 6

⅓ c. raw honey
3 tbsp. corn starch
3 c. 2% milk
¼ c. of vanilla or chocolate whey
    protein (or a scoop of each!)
Pinch of sea salt

TIP: If desired, add berries, sliced banana, or cinnamon after. Be creative!

Method

Combine all ingredients in a medium saucepan over medium low heat, whisking often until warm

Keep whisking constantly until mixture starts to boil, then for 2 more minutes or until thickened

Remove from heat and pour into a glass bowl, cover with lid or plastic wrap

Refrigerate for 2 hours

Serve

Nutrition facts per serving: Calories 145, Carbohydrates 23g, Protein 8g, Fat 3g

CHOCOLATE CHIP COOKIES

Method

Preheat oven to 350

Mix all ingredients together, adding chocolate chips and walnuts last

Use a tablespoon to scoop out batter and place on baking pan coated with non-stick spray

Bake 12-15 minutes

Place on racks and allow 5–10 minutes to cool

Nutrition facts per serving: Calories 126, Carbohydrates 19g, Protein 4g, Fat 4g

Makes 12 cookies

1 ½ c. sprouted flour
½ c. sugar + 2 tbsp.
3 eggs
½ tsp. baking powder
1 tsp. vanilla
½ tsp. sea salt
⅓ c. dark chocolate chips
¼ c. walnuts, chopped

OATMEAL COOKIES

MAKES 12 COOKIES

1 c. rolled oats
¾ c. sprouted flour
½ c. sugar
3 eggs
½ tsp. baking powder
1 tbsp. cinnamon
1 tsp. vanilla
½ tsp. nutmeg
½ tsp. sea salt
⅓ c. raisins
¼ c. pecans, chopped

Method

Preheat oven to 350

Mix ingredients together using a mixer, or a large spoon - except for oats and raisins, adding them last to the mixture

Use 2 tbsp. dough per cookie

Bake for 12-16 minutes, rotating sheets halfway through

Cool on pan for 5 minutes then place on wire racks or plate to cool completely

Nutrition facts per serving: Calories 143, Carbohydrates 24g, Protein 5g, Fat 3g

PEANUT BUTTER COOKIES

MAKES 12 COOKIES

Method

Preheat oven to 350

Mix all ingredients together in a large bowl, use a mixer if you have one, or a large spoon

Using a tablespoon, spoon out about 2 tbsp. of dough per cookie on a baking sheet coated with non-stick spray

Bake for 10-12 minutes or until golden brown

Remove from cookie sheet and cool on a rack for 5-10 minutes

Nutrition facts per serving: Calories 84, Carbohydrates 11g, Protein 5g, Fat 3g

¼ c. sugar + 2 tbsp.
¼ c. chunky peanut butter
5 egg whites
⅔ c. sprouted flour
½ tsp. baking powder
½ tsp. baking soda
½ tsp. vanilla
½ tsp. sea salt

GINGERSNAPS

MAKES 12 COOKIES

1 c. sprouted flour
2 eggs + 1 egg white
⅓ c. sugar
1 tsp. baking soda
1 ½ tsp. ground ginger
1 tsp. cinnamon
½ tsp. vanilla
¼ tsp. salt

Method

Preheat oven to 350

Mix all ingredients together in a large bowl, use a mixer if you have one, or a large spoon

Using a tablespoon, spoon out about 1 ½ tbsp. of dough per cookie on a baking sheet coated with non-stick spray

Bake for 10-12 minutes, remove from cookie sheet and cool on a rack for 5-10 minutes

Nutrition facts per serving: Calories 61, Carbohydrates 10g, Protein 3g, Fat 1g

PUMPKIN BREAD

Breads are great for breakfast, served with coffee or tea for guests, or as a snack. Enjoy these amazingly tasty AND healthy recipes...

SERVES 12

Method

Preheat oven to 350

Spray three or four 7x3 inch loaf pans with non-stick cooking spray

Mix ingredients together in a bowl and pour into loaf pans equally

Bake for 45-50 minutes

Loaves are done when inserted toothpick comes out clean

Nutrition facts per serving: Calories 198, Carbohydrates 34g, Protein 7g, Fat 4g

1 - 15 oz. can pumpkin puree
3 eggs
¾ c. applesauce
1 ¼ c. 2% milk
1 c. organic sugar
1 tbsp. coconut oil
3 ½ c. sprouted flour
2 tsp. baking soda
1 tsp. vanilla extract
1 ½ tsp. sea salt
3 tsp. cinnamon
1 tsp. nutmeg
½ tsp. ground cloves
¼ tsp. ginger

CRANBERRY BREAD

SERVES 12

2 c. sprouted flour
¾ c. organic sugar
1 tbsp. coconut oil
1 ½ tsp. baking powder
½ tsp. baking soda
1 tsp. sea salt
¾ c. fresh squeezed orange juice
    (about 3 oranges)
1 tbsp. grated orange peel
2 eggs
1 ½ c. fresh or frozen cranberries
½ c. walnuts, chopped

Method

Preheat oven to 350

Spray three or four 7x3 inch loaf pans with non-stick cooking spray

Mix ingredients together in a bowl and pour into loaf pans equally

Bake for 45-50 minutes

Loaves are done when inserted toothpick comes out clean

Nutrition facts per serving: Calories 134, Carbohydrates 22g, Protein 4g, Fat 4g

ZUCCHINI BREAD

SERVES 12

Method

Preheat oven to 350

Spray three or four 7x3 inch loaf pans with non-stick cooking spray

Mix ingredients together in a bowl and pour into loaf pans equally

Bake for 45-50 minutes

Loaves are done when inserted toothpick comes out clean

Nutrition facts per serving: Calories 190, Carbohydrates 31g, Protein 7g, Fat 5g

3 c. sprouted flour
1 ½ c. 2% milk
1 tsp. sea salt
1 tsp. baking powder
1 tsp. baking soda
3 tsp. cinnamon
3 eggs
¾ c. applesauce
1 c. organic sugar
3 tsp. vanilla extract
2 c. grated zucchini
¾ c. walnuts, chopped

BANANA BREAD

2 c. sprouted flour
¾ c. organic sugar
2 tbsp. coconut oil
½ c. applesauce
2 eggs
3 ripe bananas, thinly sliced
1 ¼ c. 2% milk
3 tsp. cinnamon
1 tsp. baking powder
1 tsp. baking soda
1 tsp. sea salt

Method

Preheat oven to 350

Spray three or four 7x3 inch loaf pans with non-stick cooking spray

Mix ingredients together in a bowl and pour into loaf pans equally

Bake for 45-50 minutes

Loaves are done when inserted toothpick comes out clean

Nutrition facts per serving: Calories 167, Carbohydrates 29g, Protein 4g, Fat 4g

BAKED APPLES

Add plain or Greek low fat yogurt with a dash of cinnamon for and extra mmmmmmmm...

SERVES 12

Method

Preheat oven to 350

Place sliced apples in a large bowl

In another bowl, mix all ingredients together

Add apples to mixture and coat all slices thoroughly

Spoon apples and mixture into a 9x13 baking dish

Bake for 50 minutes

Nutrition facts per serving: Calories 116, Carbohydrates 24g, Protein 1g, Fat 2g

6 apples, cored and sliced
6 tbsp. organic sugar
3 tbsp. sprouted flour
½ c. raisins
½ c. walnuts, chopped
½ c. 2% milk
1 tsp. vanilla
2 tsp. cinnamon
½ tsp. nutmeg
¼ tsp. cloves

GS! BERRY CRIP

Or cherry... be creative! Great with a ½ c. of plain non-fat Greek yogurt...

SERVES 15

3 c. fresh berries, strawberries, blueberries, blackberries, raspberries...
⅔ c. brown sugar, divided
1 c. applesauce, room temperature
1 ⅓ c. sprouted flour
1 ⅓ c. rolled oats
2 tsp. cinnamon
¼ tsp. ground nutmeg
½ tsp. sea salt
¼ c. organic butter or ghee, melted

Method

Preheat oven to 350

In a large bowl, gently mix berries and ⅓ c. sugar together

In another bowl, mix flour, ⅓ c. sugar, oats, cinnamon, salt and nutmeg

Mix butter and applesauce, and add in a little at a time to flour and oat mixture. Stir until crumbly, it will be moist because of the applesauce

In a 9x13 pan, press about ¾ of the flour and oat mixture into the bottom

Add berries and then sprinkle the remaining flour and oat mixture over the berries, or take a handful and evenly distribute

Bake for 35 minutes, or until fruit is bubbling and topping is golden brown

Nutrition facts per serving: Calories 180, Carbohydrates 29g, Protein 4g, Fat 6g

APPLE CINNAMON OATMEAL CRISP

Also great with a ½ c. of plain non-fat Greek yogurt...

SERVES 15

Method

Preheat oven to 350

In a large bowl, gently mix apples and ⅓ c. sugar together

In another bowl, mix flour, ⅓ c. sugar, oats, cinnamon and salt

Mix butter, vanilla and applesauce, and add in a little at a time to flour and oat mixture. Stir until crumbly, it will be moist because of the applesauce

In a 9x13 pan, press about ¾ of the flour and oat mixture into the bottom

Add apples and then sprinkle the remaining flour and oat mixture over them, or take a handful and equally distribute

Bake for 35 minutes, or until fruit is bubbling and topping is golden brown

Nutrition facts per serving: Calories 180, Carbohydrates 29g, Protein 4g, Fat 6g

⅔ c. brown sugar, divided
1 c. applesauce, room temperature
1 ⅓ c. rolled oats
1 ⅓ c. sprouted flour
¼ c. organic butter or ghee, melted
3 c. apples, cored, sliced and
  chopped
1 ½ tbsp. cinnamon
1 tsp. vanilla
½ tsp. sea salt

YELLOW CAKE & CUPCAKES

OMGoodness! ☺

SERVES 12

2 c. sprouted flour
¼ c. butter or ghee, softened or
 melted is best
1 c. organic sugar
¾ c. applesauce
¾ c. 2% milk
1 ½ tsp. vanilla extract
2 tsp. baking powder
½ tsp. salt

Method

Preheat oven to 350

Mix all ingredients in a bowl and whisk until smooth

Spray cake pan or muffin tin with non-stick baking spray

Spoon or pour cake mix into pan or tin

Bake for 15-20 minutes, or until you can insert a toothpick into the center and it comes out clean

Nutrition facts per serving: Calories 179, Carbohydrates 27g, Protein 5g, Fat 6g

FROSTING — WHITE/VANILLA OR CHOCOLATE

If you need frosting, do it right. I will whip some up and freeze it until I need it next. If making cupcakes or a big cake, use it all and double the GS! Yellow Cake recipe.

SERVES 24

Mix flour and milk (and cocoa, if making chocolate) together in a small pan. Stir and cook over medium heat until consistency is thick and smooth

To soften butter, heat up the oven and place butter in a bowl to get soft, almost melted. Mix together softened butter and honey or sugar with a mixer until creamy, then add flour mixture

Beat/mix together until no grains are left and consistency is smooth, then add 1 tsp. vanilla and mix in

Nutrition facts per serving: Calories 55, Carbohydrates 6g, Protein 1g, Fat 4g

White/Vanilla Frosting:
5 tbsp. organic white flour
1 c. 1-2% milk
6 tbsp. butter, softened
½ c. raw honey or organic sugar
1 tsp. vanilla

Chocolate Frosting:
2 tbsp. organic white flour
3 tbsp. cocoa powder
1 c. 1-2% milk
6 tbsp. butter, softened
½ c. raw honey or organic sugar
1 tsp. vanilla

CHOCOLATE CAKE & CUPCAKES

For when chocolate is needed...

SERVES 12

Method

Preheat oven to 350

Prepare cake pan or muffin tins by spraying with non-stick baking spray

Whisk or blend ingredients together

Pour into baking tin and bake for 25-35 minutes, cake is done when a toothpick is inserted and comes out clean

Let cool in pan for 5-10 minutes, then remove to rack and allow to cool completely

Frost with vanilla or chocolate frosting recipes (optional)

Nutrition facts per serving: Calories 141, Carbohydrates 26g, Protein 5g, Fat 3g

- 2 c. sprouted flour
- 1 c. organic sugar (taste batter, it should be perfect, yet if sweeter is desired try using a packet of stevia rather than adding more sugar)
- ¾ c. organic unsweetened cocoa powder, preferably 65-70% cacao
- 2 tsp. baking powder
- 1 ½ tsp. baking soda
- 1 tsp. salt
- 1 c. 2 % milk
- 2 eggs
- ½ c. applesauce
- 2 tsp. vanilla
- 1 c. boiling water

CARROT CAKE & CUPCAKES

Vegetables in cake? Oh my yes...

SERVES 12

2 c. sprouted flour
2 tsp. baking soda
½ tsp. salt
3 tsp. ground cinnamon
3 eggs
¾ c. organic sugar (taste batter, it should be perfect, yet if sweeter is desired try using a packet or two of stevia rather than adding more sugar)
¾ c. applesauce
¾ c. 2% milk
2 tsp. vanilla
2 c. carrots, grated or processed in food processor
½ c. walnuts or pecans, chopped

Method

Preheat oven to 350

Prepare cake pan or muffin tins by spraying with non-stick baking spray

Whisk or blend ingredients together

Pour into baking tin and bake for 25-35 minutes, cake is done when a toothpick is inserted and comes out clean

Let cool in pan for 5-10 minutes, then remove to rack and allow to cool completely

Frost with frosting recipes (optional) - *I like to use the warm vanilla frosting and drizzle it lightly over the cake or cupcakes* ☺

Nutrition facts per serving: Calories 168, Carbohydrates 27g, Protein 5g, Fat 4g

FRESH FROZEN FRUIT POPS

Options! Just use fruit, or use fruit and yogurt (optimal for GS! results)

SERVES 8

2 c. fresh fruit of your choice:
    berries, sliced bananas,
    pineapple, mango, etc.
2 c. plain low fat yogurt
⅛ c. honey or 1-2 packets of stevia
8 small paper cups
8 Popsicle sticks

Method

Place all ingredients into a blender and blend together to desired consistency. Taste and adjust sweetness if necessary

Pour contents into each paper cup, filling almost all the way up, leave about ½ inch from top

Cover all 8 cups with wax paper, cling wrap, or aluminum foil and poke Popsicle sticks through

Freeze for 4-5 hours

Nutrition facts per serving: Calories 71, Carbohydrates 14g, Protein 3g, Fat 1g

Also try:

Yogurt Pops – Same as above with 1 tsp. each of vanilla extract and cinnamon

Protein Pops, Vanilla/Chocolate or both! – Freeze Power Pudding recipe the same way!

Rule #10: Love yourself

Be good to yourself, this is loving yourself. By giving your body what it <u>truly</u> needs, you will be better to and for others.

MEASUREMENT EQUIVALENTS

Volume (Dry)

American Standard	Metric
⅛ teaspoon	.5 ml
¼ teaspoon	1 ml
½ teaspoon	2 ml
¾ teaspoon	4 ml
1 teaspoon	5 ml
1 tablespoon	15 ml
¼ cup	59 ml
⅓ cup	79 ml
½ cup	118 ml
⅔ cup	158 ml
¾ cup	177 ml
1 cup	225 ml
2 cups or 1 pint	450 ml
3 cups	675 ml
4 cups or 1 quart	1 liter
½ gallon	2 liters
1 gallon	4 liters

Oven Temperatures

American Standard	Metric
250° F	130° C
300° F	150° C
350° F	180° C
400° F	200° C
450° F	230° C

Weight (Mass)

American Standard (Ounces)	Metric (Grams)
½ ounce	15 grams
1 ounce	30 grams
3 ounces	85 grams
3.75 ounces	100 grams
4 ounces	115 grams
8 ounces	225 grams
12 ounces	340 grams
16 ounces or 1 pound	450 grams

Volume (Liquid)

American Standard (Cups & Quarts)	American Standard (Ounces)	Metric (Milliliters & Liters)
2 tbsp	1 fl. oz.	30 ml
¼ cup	2 fl. oz.	60 ml
½ cup	4 fl. oz.	125 ml
1 cup	8 fl. oz.	250 ml
1 ½ cups	12 fl. oz.	375 ml
2 cups or 1 pint	16 fl. oz.	500 ml
4 cups or 1 quart	32 fl. oz.	1000 ml or 1 liter
1 gallon	128 fl. oz.	4 liters

Dry Measure Equivalents

3 teaspoons	1 tablespoon	½ ounce	14.3 grams
2 tablespoons	⅛ cup	1 ounce	28.3 grams
4 tablespoons	¼ cup	2 ounces	56.7 grams
5 ⅓ tablespoons	⅓ cup	2.6 ounces	75.6 grams
8 tablespoons	½ cup	4 ounces	113.4 grams
12 tablespoons	¾ cup	6 ounces	.375 pound
32 tablespoons	2 cups	16 ounces	1 pound

British and American Variances

Term	Abbreviation	Nationality	Dry or liquid	Metric equivalent	Equivalent in context
cup	c., C.		usually liquid	237 milliliters	16 tablespoons or 8 ounces
ounce	fl oz, fl. oz.	American	liquid only	29.57 milliliters	
		British	either	28.41 milliliters	
gallon	gal.	American	liquid only	3.785 liters	4 quarts
		British	either	4.546 liters	4 quarts
inch	in, in.			2.54 centimeters	
ounce	oz, oz.	American	dry	28.35 grams	1⁄16 pound
			liquid	see OUNCE	see OUNCE
pint	p., pt.	American	liquid	0.473 liter	1⁄8 gallon or 16 ounces
			dry	0.551 liter	1⁄2 quart
		British	either	0.568 liter	
pound	lb.		dry	453.592 grams	16 ounces
quart	q., qt, qt.	American	liquid	0.946 liter	1⁄4 gallon or 32 ounces
			dry	1.101 liters	2 pints
		British	either	1.136 liters	
teaspoon	t., tsp., tsp		either	about 5 milliliters	1⁄3 tablespoon
tablespoon	T., tbs., tbsp.		either	about 15 milliliters	3 teaspoons or 1⁄2 ounce

INDEX

bold denotes photo

A

American Medical Association, xiii
Andrew's Mexican Salmon Sandwich, **49**, 73
Apple Cinnamon Oatmeal Crisp, 155
Asian
    Asian Chicken Lettuce Wraps, **xxv**, 31
    Beef and Broccoli, 115
    Chinese Chicken and Mushrooms, 114
    Chinese Chicken Salad, **48**, 53
    Lo Mein, 121
    Stir Fry, 113
    Thai Chicken Satay, 119
    Vegetable Fried Rice, 120
Asian Chicken Lettuce Wraps, **xxv**, 31

B

bad food, eliminating of from your house, xvi
Baked Apples, 153
Baked Chicken Tenders & Fish Sticks, 83
Baked Fish, 98
Baked White Fish with Pesto Sauce, 89
Baked Ziti, 109–110
balance, importance of, xv
Banana Bread, 152
BBC Breakfast-Bake-Casserole, **x**, 20
BBQ Chicken Salad, 56
beans
    Beans and Greens, 129
    Black Bean Burgers, 70
    Quinoa and Black Bean Salad, 134
    Refried Beans with Cheese (optional), 93
    Spicy Black Bean Dip, 36
    White Bean and Basil Hummus, 34
Beans and Greens, 129
Beef and Broccoli, 115

Beer Batter Fish Tacos, 87
Biscuits, 139
Black Bean Burgers, 70
breads
    Banana Bread, 152
    Biscuits, 139
    Cornbread, 140
    Cranberry Bread, 150
    Mmmmmm – Muffins (3 Ways! At Least …), 23
    Pumpkin Bread, 149
    Zucchini Bread, 151
Breakfast Tacos, 14
breakfasts
    BBC Breakfast Bake Casserole, **x**, 20
    Breakfast Tacos, 14
    Frittata, 17–18
    GS! Egg Sandwich, 13
    GS! Power-full Shake, 3
    Mmmmmm – Muffins (3 Ways! At Least …), 23
    Muesli, **ix**, 5
    My True Nutrition Huevos Rancheros, 24
    Nancy's Fabulous French Toast, 22
    Oh My GS! Omelet, 15
    Parfait, **viii**, 7
    Perfect Protein Pancakes or Waffles 5 Ways, 9–10
    Protein Oatmeal with Fruit and Nuts, 4
    Protein Packed Granola, **viii**, 6, 42
    Scrambled Eggs & Veggie Scramble, 12
    Simple Chewy Cereal Protein Bars, **x**, 8
    Smoked Salmon with Eggs, **ix**, 16
    Spinach Bacon Feta Wrap, 19
Bruschetta, 37
burgers
    Black Bean Burgers, 70
    GS! Simply Hamburgers, 68
    Mahi Burgers, 72

Printed in the United States
By Bookmasters